CW01648777

Quiet word 2

Fully worked-out programmes
for quiet days and reflective events

NICK FAWCETT

kevin
mayhew

kevin mayhew

First published in Great Britain in 2011 by Kevin Mayhew Ltd
Buxhall, Stowmarket, Suffolk IP14 3BW
Tel: +44 (0) 1449 737978 Fax: +44 (0) 1449 737834
E-mail: info@kevinmayhewltd.com

www.kevinmayhew.com

9 8 7 6 5 4 3 2 1 0

ISBN 978 1 84867 431 8
Catalogue No. 1501304

Cover design by Rob Mortonson
© Image used under licence from Shutterstock Inc.
Proofread by Rebecca Henning
Typeset by Richard Weaver

Printed and bound in Great Britain

Contents

Foreword

During my time as a minister in Cheltenham, a local church asked me to lead a Quiet Day. It was an unremarkable request, except that I had no experience of leading or sharing in such an event, so was unsure what to do or expect. As a result, what I produced wasn't so much a Quiet Day (the programme providing insufficient time for silence) as a reflective event, using slides, music, readings and meditations to promote prayerful consideration of the person and message of Jesus. The day was nonetheless well received, and led to many other similar events using such media, each aimed at engaging the senses and imagination in worship. In time, these were published as fully worked-out programmes under the title *A Quiet Word*, drawn from the two volumes of my book *No Ordinary Man*.

This compilation brings together in a single volume, and in an accessible format designed for ease of use, the Quiet Day programmes – complete with appropriate meditations – from the three recently published volumes of *A Most Amazing Man* (reproduced in non-Lectionary form as *A Man Like No Other*), each of which focuses exclusively on the Gospel accounts of the birth, life, death and resurrection of Christ. The purpose of each event is the same: to encourage people to reflect on the person of Jesus, prompting them to ask: 'Who was this man?' 'What did he do?' 'Why did he do it?' And, above all, 'What does he mean for me today?'

Whether you decide to use the suggested audio-visual material is up to you; it depends on whether you are looking to stage a Quiet Day per se – in which case you possibly won't – or a more varied reflective event. Assuming the latter, there are a few points to consider in addition to those listed under Practical Matters (see next section). Many of the slide collections (see the Appendix) are very hard to get hold of today but, with ever-changing technology and corresponding resource material being produced, you may be able to find – via an online search – the same or similar material in PowerPoint format. If you do make use of the slides, you will need to go through them carefully and select those that most effectively complement each reading and meditation. You may, instead, decide to use just the suggested music. An effective way of presenting this is to fade the volume after an interval so that the relevant Scripture passage can be read over it, before bringing the volume back up and continuing to the end of the piece. Should slides be used, these are best shown in conjunction with the music and reading.

Whichever option you go for, be sure to allow plenty of time for silence which, as you will see, is integral to each of the events outlined here. In an age where life seems to be lived at an ever more frenetic pace, we all need time to pause and reflect. It is my hope that the material in this book may prove helpful in affording such an opportunity.

Nick Fawcett

Practical matters

Should you choose to use the audiovisual material suggested in this book, there are obviously certain basic requirements. A good hi-fi system, slide projector and screen are essential, as is an effective amplification system so that readers can be heard over any background music. You will also find the services of an assistant invaluable when it comes to presenting the material – ideally somebody to control the slide projector, and possibly someone to fade the music in and out as appropriate. Remember, too, to ensure that those reading the meditations are given proper time to prepare beforehand, and that they are instructed to read slowly and clearly, beginning by announcing the title of the meditation.

You can probably borrow much of the recommended music from your local library or a friend. Should you prefer to buy it, much is available on budget CD sets. I made particular use of *The Voices of Angels (100 Heavenly Classics), 100 Romantic Classics, 100 Relaxing Classics* and *100 Popular Classics,* (Castle Communications); *Discovering the Classics* (three-volume, double-CD set), *Renaissance Choral Treasures* and *Classical Favourites for Relaxing and Dreaming* (Naxos); the *Classic Experience* discs 1 and 3 (EMI); and Classic FM's *All Time Christmas Greats*. Other works extensively used are Handel's *Messiah,* Mozart's *Requiem, Mass in C minor* and *Coronation Mass,* and the various compositions of Margaret Rizza and Keith Duke, available from Kevin Mayhew Publishers.

Slide collections are not easy to find nowadays. You may be able to buy or hire some (see the Appendix), but many, sadly, are out of print. Your best bet may be to borrow them from your local Diocesan Resource Centre if you have one. Failing that, you might once more try your local library. When using slides, always run through them beforehand to make sure they are the right way up and in the correct order. Ensure also that you have a spare bulb in case one should blow, and arrange all electrical leads so that no one can inadvertently fall over them. The less you leave to chance, the less possibility there will be of anything going wrong.

One final point: the material here makes extensive use of music, meditations, readings and visual images, but equally important, as stated in the Foreword, is the place of silence. Do not neglect this. Participants need time to reflect on what they have heard and seen if God is to speak through it. I have indicated opportunities for silent reflection at numerous points throughout the sessions. Encourage people to make the most of these times, and to respect the space and quiet of other participants.

Quiet Days

Reflective events

The God who is always with us

Suggested visual material

Jesus of Nazareth 6
The Life of Christ IV

FIRST SESSION

Introduction

'They shall name him Emmanuel, which means "God is with us"' – the promise given to Joseph by the angel in his dream. But what does that mean? In what way, through Christ, do we directly experience God's presence? It's easy to use such language, but is it anything more than jargon? How far, in other words, is it backed up in daily life? That's what we're going to consider today, reflecting on words of Scripture to ask whether it makes sense to speak of knowing God personally, here by our side and, if so, exploring ways in which we can deepen that awareness.

Opening prayer

Living God,
you are near to us,
yet we stray far from your side.
You reach out,
and we push you away.
You call,
and we ignore.
You embrace,
and we resist.
But in our hearts we long for you,
our hearts being restless without your peace.

We crave your guidance, strength, help and forgiveness,
even while we deny our need.
Reveal yourself afresh to us in Christ,
fill us again with your Spirit.
Enfold us once more in your love,
and help us to recognise your presence beside and within us.
Come now,
and open our hearts to you.
Amen.

Music *(optional)*

Let not your hearts be troubled (In God Alone) Andrew Moore

Reading

John 14:1-14

Comment

If God is with us in Christ, then you'd have thought, wouldn't you, that his disciples of all people would have recognised it? They, surely, would have seen and understood the truth. But no. Take a look at the four Gospels and you'll see that for a considerable time – in fact, for almost the whole extent of Jesus' earthly ministry – they walked and talked with him yet failed to grasp the truth of who he was. He'd shown them what God is like, revealed his love, yet – as we'll see in a moment in our reading – still they could ask him, 'Show us the Father.' It was only after Jesus' death and resurrection that they finally realised that in this amazing man they had encountered God himself.

As John puts it at the start of his Gospel: 'We have seen his glory, the glory as of a father's only son, full of grace and truth.' What is the lesson here? Perhaps simply this: that we are not always aware of what's staring us in the face, often needing the benefit of hindsight before the truth dawns. Or perhaps this: that we tend to see only what we're looking for. Look instead to Christ – his words and deeds, life and death as recorded in Scripture – and be open to what they say concerning God . . . and you.

Meditation of Philip

'Show us the Father,' I asked.
Can you believe that!
After three years of following Jesus,
three years of walking by his side,
still I could come up with a daft line like that!
It makes me cringe now to think of it,
but at the time,
despite all he'd said,
it seemed perfectly sensible,
the most natural request in the world.
I was coming at things the wrong way, you see,
wanting all my questions answered –
as though I could understand everything about God,
all there is to know,
down to the very last detail.
And I'd no need –
that's the stupid thing –
for I'd seen him already,
there by my side in Jesus.
In his words,
his deeds,
his love,
his mercy,
God was present –
like Father, like Son,
the Word made flesh –
but I couldn't see for looking,
the wood obscured by the trees.
Learn from my mistake,
or you may search eagerly for God
yet never find.
We'll never understand *everything*,
not in this life,
not until we see him face to face,
but in Jesus we've seen enough and more than enough:
all we need to know.

Quiet reflection

Prayer

Almighty God,
thank you that, for all your splendour,
all your majesty, power and glory,
we can not only know *about* you
but know you *personally*,
your greatness having been revealed in Christ,
your purpose fulfilled through him.
Thank you for, through him, bringing the divine down to earth,
making it real for us in such a way that we can see and understand it,
relating who and what you are to our daily lives.
Help us, if we would know you better,
to focus our thoughts on Jesus,
one with us yet one also with you.
Amen.

Silence

Music *(optional)*

Prayer of St Teresa (Awakening in Love) Margaret Rizza

Reading

John 14:15-21

Comment

God revealed through Christ. That's all very well, you may say, but we're at a major disadvantage, for his early followers knew him in the flesh, followed him through the streets of Galilee during the course of his earthly ministry, and met him again as the risen Lord in the days after his resurrection. It's different for us, for we're denied that privilege of seeing him face to face, of having someone tangible we can relate to first-hand. And, of course, that's absolutely true, so far as it goes . . . only it doesn't go far enough. Admittedly, Jesus is not physically here by our side, but he is with us nonetheless in a way more special still: present through his Spirit deep within our hearts. Listen again to his promise – to you and to all.

Meditation of the Apostle John

We felt abandoned,
bereft –
like orphans in a hostile and dangerous world.
To see Jesus arrested like that,
flogged, crucified and laid in a tomb –
it was like losing a parent, partner and friend all in one,
for we'd loved him beyond all others,
his presence giving meaning to life,
light to our path.
But then he returned,
just as he'd promised –
risen,
victorious,
yet the same old Jesus we'd known before.
He walked with us,
talked with us,
and for a moment it was as though nothing had happened.
But it *had*, of course,
for he'd defeated death,
vanquished evil,
his place no longer with *us* but with the Father,
enthroned on high.
He knew it,
we knew it,
and so it proved,
our Lord taken from us again . . .
but we're not abandoned,
not alone,

for once more,
just as he promised,
he's present among us,
his Spirit within,
to the end of time.

Quiet reflection

Prayer

Saviour Christ,
thank you for the promise of your return,
the knowledge that, in the fullness of time,
you will come again to establish your kingdom
and to welcome all your people, from every place and time,
into the joy of your kingdom.
But thank you also that you have come again already,
not just in the miracle of your resurrection
but in the equally miraculous gift of your Holy Spirit,
dwelling within,
making you known.
Thank you for, through that Spirit,
touching our hearts and transforming our lives –
enabling,
inspiring,
teaching,
guiding –
bringing faith to birth
and sustaining it across the years.
Open our hearts to the Spirit's work,
and make us wholly yours.
Amen.

Silent retreat

SECOND SESSION

Comment

Through his Spirit, Jesus tells us, God is with us, deep within. It sounds good, but what does it mean? Sadly, the person of the Holy Spirit has been the subject of untold controversy within the Church, too often causing suspicion, hostility, bitterness and division – the very opposite of what God intended. Why has this happened? Because we try to pin down what cannot be fully identified, to define what defies labels, thus closing our hearts to what we imagine we accept. We forget that the Spirit blows where it will, mighty and mysterious. Yet of course, if this really is God at work within us, how could it be anything other than beyond words or understanding, beyond any attempt on our part to fit the divine into neat human categories? We do not understand the how, where or when, nor do we need to understand. What we know and experience is a sense of God's inner prompting and presence; his Spirit with us now.

Music *(optional)*

Dance in the spirit (Music for Lent, Holy Week and Easter) Keith Duke

Reading

John 20:19-23

Meditation of James

A mighty wind, some point to,
tongues of fire,
as though *that* was the moment the Spirit came,
dramatic and unmistakable.
They're half right of course,
for that Pentecost experience *was* special,
transforming not only our lives,
but also the world,
for ever.

Yet the turning point came earlier,
when, as we huddled behind locked doors,
lost and fearful,
Jesus appeared from nowhere and breathed new life –
resurrection life –
into our hearts.
No fuss,
no fireworks,
but suddenly we felt different –
energised and enthused,
yet also strangely tranquil,
at peace with ourselves and with God.
It was part of his special gift,
his presence within us,
teaching,
guiding,
enabling,
inspiring:
one moment, signs and wonders,
the next, quiet nurture;
one minute, sending us out,
the next, working within.
You can't tie it down,
nor should you try,
for the Spirit blows where it wills,
poured out on us,
on you,
on all:
a gust of wind yet a gentle breeze,
a breath of fresh air,
God's kiss of life.

Quiet reflection

Prayer

Mighty God,
we praise you for the activity, experience and power of your Spirit,
making real your presence within our hearts.

We celebrate how, through that Spirit,
you give us guidance, instruction and insight;
how you challenge and inspire,
nurturing and nourishing our faith
and equipping us for service.
Above all, we rejoice that the Spirit works,
not according to our own wishes –
directed by any merit, deserving or ingenuity on our part –
but directed by your will,
moving at your behest and fulfilling your purpose.
Fill, renew, shape and transform us,
to the glory of your name.
Amen.

Silence

Comment

So then, God is with us as Father, Son and Holy Spirit. But we've yet to touch on perhaps the most celebrated and certainly most direct statement on the subject in the Bible: the verse in Matthew's Gospel in which Jesus promises that where two or three are gathered in his name, he is there among them. In what sense, do you think, did he mean that? Is it simply that his Spirit is especially able to move, or his words come uniquely to life in such a situation, or was he saying something more? Other words of Jesus indicate very much the latter, for he talked repeatedly of speaking through *our* lips, working through *our* hands, reaching out through *our* lives. By sharing together, worshipping together, serving together, we somehow make Christ present in our midst, and if that's so it brings with it a challenge as well as promise, for it implies that for Jesus to minister effectively to our world it needs *us* to play our part as much as *him* to play his. That's a wonderful, but daunting, thought.

Music *(optional)*

You, Lord, are in this place (Sacred Weave) Keith Duke

Reading

Matthew 18:15-20

Meditation of Matthew

He said he'd be there, however small our numbers,
present among us if we met in his name.
And he *was* at first,
when, as we huddled behind locked doors,
he appeared among us,
risen,
victorious,
alive!
It was wonderful,
breathtaking,
all the more so, given that he'd been dead and buried,
for we honestly thought we'd said goodbye.
Suddenly he was with us again,
our friend Jesus,
and we assumed it would stay like that for ever.
Only it wasn't to be,
for once more he was taken away,
transported before our very eyes,
and when we next met together,
gathered for prayer and worship,
we waited to see him in vain.
He'll come, I said,
give him time,
but days turned to weeks . . .
weeks to months . . .
and he didn't.
Or at least, so we thought,
but of course we were wrong,
for as we broke bread and shared wine,
he was there,
as we read from the Scriptures,
he was there,
as we ministered to others in word and deed,

he was there,
his Spirit with us in all we did,
and I've come to understand what I should have grasped before:
that those words of his weren't just promising *he'd* be there for *us* –
that could be taken as read –
but were also asking whether *we'd* be there for *him*!

Quiet reflection

Prayer

Risen Lord,
teach us that though you are enthroned on high
you are also close by our sides;
though you are far off
you are also near;
though you have left us in the flesh
you are with us in the Spirit.
Help us to recognise your presence through worship and reflection;
to glimpse your glory in the world around us;
to hear your call in the cry of the needy;
and, above all, to meet and greet you in the fellowship of your people,
celebrating the truth that
where two or three are gathered in your name,
you are there indeed amongst them,
just as you promised to be.
Amen.

Silent retreat

Closing comment

God with us: wishful thinking, or a daily reality? For many, God is seen as remote and distant, set apart in splendid isolation much as he's so often depicted in the Old Testament. For others he's some vague yet looming presence; a stern and often angry deity looking over people's shoulders to make sure they don't step out of line, and waiting to punish them if they do. For others he's some elemental force, real enough yet altogether impersonal. The God proclaimed in the gospel is very different, his face being revealed in the life, death and resurrection of Christ; his presence experienced through the indwelling of his Spirit and fellowship of his people; his call reaching us through those we meet here in the world around us. He is here by our side, living within, at work in our lives – a God both far and near.

Closing prayer

Thank you, Lord, that, seen or unseen,
known or unbeknown,
accepted or rejected,
you are there.
Thank you that, in good or bad,
joy or sorrow,
hope or fear,
life or death,
you are there.
Thank you that, whoever we are,
whatever we do,
wherever we might be,
once again, you are there.
Help us, in turn, to be there for you.
Amen.

Promise and fulfilment

Suggested visual material

Jesus of Nazareth 2 and 3
The Life of Christ II

FIRST SESSION

Introduction

Read the Gospel accounts of the life, death and resurrection of Jesus and one thing will leap out at you: the constant references to events taking place in order to fulfil the Scriptures. In the opening four chapters of Matthew alone there are four examples, and so it continues through the remaining chapters. Words of the Law and prophets are seen to point beyond their original context to the ministry of Christ, finding there a deeper relevance. But is this what we mean by the fulfilment of God's word? In part, yes, for it reminds us that he is always at work in ways we have barely begun to imagine. But, as we will explore today, what Jesus meant by fulfilment of Scripture went much deeper, taking us to the heart of God's promises and the ultimate realisation of his purpose. We will start with his own words concerning the Law and prophets, before moving on in our second session to some of the questions *we* may have as to what fulfilment means.

Opening prayer

Loving God,
we remember how, across the centuries,
you have been faithful to your people,
honouring your promises of old.
You told Abraham that, through his seed,
all the earth would be blessed . . .
and so it was.

You told Moses that you would lead the Israelites out of Egypt,
through the wilderness to the Promised Land . . .
and so you did.
You told the prophets of a messiah
who would deliver us from our sins . . .
and you came to our world in Christ.
You told the apostles that, though he would die,
he would rise again . . .
and, once more, so it proved.
Teach us that, though there is much in life we do not understand,
and though fulfilment of your promises sometimes seems slow,
we need to put our trust in you,
keeping faith that though *we* fail *you*,
you will stay true to *us*.
Amen.

Comment

There are times when, if we are to understand something properly, we must look at the bigger picture rather than focus on incidental details. So it is with Christ's fulfilment of the Law and prophets. Yes, the details here matter, as we will see later in this session, but it's what both of these are ultimately all about that concerned Jesus most: bridging the gap between God and humankind, and dealing with what keeps us apart. The old way did so through complex rituals and sacrifice; *he* came to offer himself. The law prescribed outward observance; *he* brought inner change. And even as they fumed against him, plotting his downfall, the guardians of the old covenant were inadvertently preparing the way for the new. That which the commandments were designed to achieve, and which they longed for the Messiah to bring, had dawned in Christ; God's promise was about to be fulfilled, though few at the time would recognise it. So often what we see depends on what we're looking for, even when it comes to the things of God.

Music *(optional)*

Agnus Dei (Requiem) Fauré

Reading

Matthew 5:13-20

Meditation of a scribe

I've come, he said, not to abolish the Law,
but to fulfil it.
What gall!
What impudence!
To suggest, even in passing, that anyone –
let alone this peasant,
this nobody from the sticks –
can add to God's commands,
enlarging on what they mean.
Blasphemy, I call it,
and I should know,
for I've spent my life studying the Scriptures,
poring over the fine print to understand every nuance,
every jot and tittle,
down to the very last detail.
It's a complex business,
everything needing to be just so:
the right rituals followed and sacrifices made
if we're to atone for our sins,
escape punishment
and find favour with God.
So does this Jesus fellow realise what he's saying –
that all this,
the requirements of the Law,
can be replaced by one man;
that our mistakes can be miraculously dealt with
and our punishment taken away
through anything he might do?
I tell you, people have died for saying less,
and, mark my words, he's heading the same way,
but he doesn't seem to care,
almost as though he feels that killing him would prove his point.

Well, let him carry on if he wants to –
it's *his* funeral.
Let him die if he must –
tried and condemned by the Law he claims to fulfil –
and we'll see what that achieves, won't we!

Quiet reflection

Prayer

Lord, we've heard it so many times:
that the requirements of the Law are fulfilled in *you*,
summed up in two commands –
to love you and love one another.
Yet though we know this in theory,
in practice it's another matter.
Still we turn faith into a matter of rules and regulations,
and still we have an uneasy sense
that you're looking over our shoulder
hungry to enforce them:
swift to condemn,
eager to punish.
Help us to understand that this is *our* way,
not *yours*;
a caricature of faith shaped by our fears rather than your grace.
And, realising that truth,
may we begin to grasp the depth of your love
and extent of your mercy,
so that we might celebrate the freedom you offer us in Christ,
the fullness of life he died to bring.
Amen.

Silence

Comment

If the heart and intentions of the Law are fulfilled in Christ, does that mean it no longer has any relevance to us; that we can forget everything it teaches so long as we walk the way of love? Put simply, yes, only of course that begs the question: what does love involve? And, properly understood, the Law offers teaching on precisely that. Nowhere do we see this more clearly than in the Sermon on the Mount, where Jesus takes first one commandment, then another, then others still, each time pointing to a deeper meaning exemplified through him. Turning the other cheek, giving to those in need, shining as a light to the world, loving one's enemies – in Jesus we see faith put into practice, deeds matching words, taking us beyond the letter to the spirit of the Law, to what God truly desires: his promises of old finally fulfilled.

Music *(optional)*

Gloria (Missa Solemnis) Mozart

Reading

Matthew 5:21-37

Meditation of a listener to the Sermon on the Mount

We were shocked at first,
truly horrified,
to hear him speaking like that about the Law,
one point after another,
giving a wholly different slant on what we'd always believed.
'You have heard it was said . . .' he told us.
'But I say to you . . .'
And then he effectively rewrote the Scriptures,
almost as though he were God himself.
Well, call me old-fashioned, but it was hard to swallow,
for I'd been brought up to respect our elders,
those who'd spent their lives studying sacred things,
so I dug my heels in,
unwilling even to give him a hearing,
let alone consider his words.

I'd shut them out,
or so I thought,
but I hadn't,
for somehow they took hold despite me,
not only asking ultimate questions
but also providing the answers.
Like it or not,
his teaching made sense,
cutting to the heart of the matter,
and, contrary to first impressions,
he didn't deny the past but fulfilled it,
showing how everything that *has been*
leads up to what *is* and *yet shall be.*
He's given fresh meaning to the Law and prophets,
and, more than that, to life itself,
revealing a purpose to it all
and showing the way we should take.
How did I put it just now?
'Almost as though he were God himself.'
Ridiculous, I know,
but it makes you think, doesn't it!

Quiet reflection

Prayer

Father God,
we read of Jesus being the fulfilment of the Law and prophets,
the consummation of your word of old,
but too often we pay lip service to that idea,
having little if any real conception of what it means,
or forgetting to apply it in practice.
Teach us whenever we read and study the Scriptures,
whenever we hear them proclaimed,
to consider them in the light of Christ,
measuring what we find there against his love,
his compassion,

his mercy
and his openness to all.
Save us from being so bound to dogma, doctrine or tradition
that we end up worshipping words on a page
or ideas in our mind
rather than your Son,
the risen Lord and King of kings.
Through him,
help us to hear your voice,
discern your presence
and know your will.
Amen.

Silent retreat

SECOND SESSION

Comment

God's promises, so we believe, can be relied on. But for all of us it's hard at times not to doubt that. We look at our lives or at the world, and wonder why God fails to act as we expect, why our prayers seemingly go unanswered. That's precisely what John the Baptist felt centuries ago as, having baptised the one he believed to be the Messiah, he subsequently found himself locked away in prison with the future looking bleak. What had gone wrong, he wondered? Had he mistaken his man, or, worse still, were God's promises not as solid as he'd hoped? It must have been with questions such as those on his mind that he sent some of his followers to find out what was going on.

Music *(optional)*

Come, my Lord, my light, my way (Sacred Weave) Keith Duke

Reading

Matthew 11:2-11

Meditation of John the Baptist

'Are you the one?' I asked.
'The one we've been waiting for,
yearning for,
across the centuries?'
I should have known, you say,
without need of confirmation,
but remember, I'd been locked up in prison for months
with no news of anything or anyone,
and it was hard to understand why God had let that happen,
let alone for me to keep faith in the future.
What if I'd been wrong,
mistaken the signs?
What if the man I'd baptised wasn't the Messiah after all,
the chosen one of God?
It could all have been some ghastly mistake,
and, in my dark, dank cell, that thought had begun to haunt me.
So when word filtered through that Jesus was at work,
his words creating a stir,
naturally I wanted to know more,
to gauge whether my first impressions had been right
and not some deluded dream.
I sent out my followers to learn more,
and the news they brought me said it all –
of the blind able to see,
the lame to walk,
lepers made whole
and the dead raised;
of good news for the poor,
justice for the weak
and hope for the oppressed –
ancient promises fulfilled at last.
I remain a captive of course,
I'd expected that,

but I'm free nonetheless,
for the one I'd longed to see had come at last,
bringing liberty to all.
I'd lived to see the dawn of his kingdom.
Now, if necessary, I was ready to die for it, too.

Quiet reflection

Prayer

Loving God,
for the countless ways you've transformed people's lives,
restoring and renewing,
we praise you.
For giving strength to the weak,
hope to the oppressed,
freedom to those held captive
and healing to the sick,
we worship you.
For bringing joy to the sorrowful,
peace to the troubled,
and light to those in darkness,
we thank you.
And, above all,
for conquering evil with good,
hatred with love
and death with life,
we honour and acclaim you.
Humbly and gratefully, we offer our lives to your service
and for the work of your kingdom.
Amen.

Silence

Comment

John the Baptist discovered that God *was* being faithful to his promises, even though for a time that was hard to see. His own situation seemed to count against it, masking the truth, yet even while things had seemed hopeless, God had been at work, the kingdom having dawned in Christ just as John had dared to believe. But where is that kingdom now, we might ask, as – two thousand years on – we look at our world and see it racked by the same greed, hatred, evil and need that dogged it then? If it dawned with Jesus, shouldn't it have grown by now? Shouldn't there be signs of its presence all around us? Again, with John, we might ask, what's happening; what's gone wrong? Especially so when we read passages like the one we're going to hear now from Matthew's Gospel, which seem to imply that his kingdom would be established within the lifetime of his hearers. Can we make sense of the apparent discrepancy, or must we conclude that God's promises are somehow flawed; even, dare we say it, wishful thinking? It's to questions such as those that we now turn.

Music *(optional)*

Creator God (River of Peace) Margaret Rizza

Reading

Matthew 24:30-35

Meditation of a second-century Jewish Christian

I'm not just *struggling* with what he said;
I'm hopelessly at sea.
For he implied that everything he foretold would soon be fulfilled,
if not in the lifetime of those present
then at least within their generation –
the Son of Man appearing in power and glory
to gather his people from the four winds.
And that wasn't all, of course,
for he spoke also of portents in heaven
and signs on earth –
clear and unmistakable indications that the day of the Lord is at hand.
Well, where are they?

Do *you* see them?
I don't.
Yet already a generation has come and gone,
consigned to history, along with their hopes and fears.
Was Jesus wrong, then, in what he said?
Did he get his wires crossed,
his dates muddled?
It's hard not to think so,
for terrible times have come and gone,
and where was Jesus when we needed him?
Our city was destroyed,
the Temple demolished,
our people scattered across the face of the earth.
But though we cried out in despair,
begged him to rescue us,
we seemed to be praying in vain.
Yet don't be fooled,
for he *did* hear,
and did answer,
giving us strength and hope
even in our darkest moments.
Throughout it all he's been with us,
here through his Spirit,
to comfort,
inspire,
lead,
provide,
his word staying true though all else fails.
And it's not just *one* generation that can experience that;
it's *every* generation,
all of us assured that, whatever life may bring,
our eternal future is secure.
Through his dying and rising again,
his coming among us and returning to the Father,
he's done everything that needs to be done,
reconciling us with God once and for all.
The denouement is yet to come,
the final chord in the grand finale still to be played,

but to those with eyes to see and ears to hear
his kingdom has dawned,
his victory is won
and his word endures for ever.
His kingdom is near,
for *he* is near.
What more do we need to know!

Quiet reflection

Prayer

Eternal God,
instil in us a vision of your eternal kingdom,
a sense of anticipation at the joys you hold in store.
Teach us to look forward in confidence
to that day when you will gather your people
from the ends of the earth,
from every place and time,
welcoming us, with them, into your presence.
But save us from being so full of heaven
that we are of no earthly use,
dismissing this world and abandoning our responsibilities towards it
through dwelling unduly on the world to come.
Remind us, should we forget,
that though the fulfilment of your purpose lies in the future,
you are working here and now,
each of us, through your Spirit,
having tasted your blessing
and glimpsed the dawn of your kingdom.
Teach us to trust in what you *will* do
and to celebrate what you are doing already.
Amen.

Silent retreat

Closing comment

What God has promised, he will do: that's the message of Scripture. And we believe it to be true since so much of what he promised has already been done. The one promised to Abraham, prefigured in the Law and anticipated by the prophets, entered our world in Christ, giving his life and bearing our sins, just as it was foretold. The true meaning of the commandments has been unfolded through him, and across the centuries generations of Christians have found his word to be true, his assurances dependable. Not that everything is clear to us, life working out precisely as we hope and expect, for *our* thoughts are not God's thoughts nor his ways our ways, but on the basis of what we have seen we trust in what is unseen; through what we have experienced we put our faith in his eternal future. What God has promised will be fulfilled, in this life or the next.

Closing prayer

Teach us, Lord, in the light of what we know,
what we have experienced,
what we have found to be true,
to trust when we do not know,
when we struggle to understand,
when life proves a puzzle to which we cannot find an answer.
Remembering what you have done,
and rejoicing in what you do now,
help us to keep faith in what you hold in store,
through Jesus Christ our Lord.
Amen.

Faith in action

Suggested visual material

Jesus of Nazareth 3 and 4
The Life of Christ II

FIRST SESSION

Introduction

One deed is worth a thousand speeches, says an old American proverb. Another says, one good deed can change the world. And all of us, of course, will be familiar with the idea of doing our good deed for the day. But do we actually do it? That's the question. And it's one that lies at the very heart of our faith. Look at the teaching of Jesus, and indeed at Scripture as a whole – both Old Testament and New – and we see emphasised time and again the need to translate words into deeds, faith into action. Yes, we're saved through faith, not works, and no, all the good deeds in the world cannot justify us before God, but that doesn't mean they're an optional extra, incidental to Christian discipleship. True love of God will show itself in love of others; serving him showing itself through loving them. We must practise what we preach if it's actually to mean anything, much as God did in Christ, his word becoming flesh; living, loving and dying among us; expressing itself in selfless sacrifice and renewing grace. It's not enough to know the jargon or talk up the gospel; if faith is to be more than simply words we must live it out, showing that we mean what we say.

Opening prayer

Gracious God,
we thank you that you didn't just *talk* about love,
but showed it in action,

entering our world in Christ,
and enduring suffering and death to bring us life.
We thank you that, through him,
you strengthened the weak,
healed the sick,
comforted the sorrowful
and redeemed the lost,
bringing good news to the poor,
hope to the oppressed
and acceptance to the outcast.
Help us, in turn, to live in such a way
that our deeds and words are one –
that what we profess with our lips we express in our lives.
Teach us your way,
and help us to follow.
Amen.

Comment

Distinctive discipleship – that, in a nutshell, is what Jesus asks for from his followers. And such distinctiveness comes not through faithfulness in worship, or soundness of doctrine, or uprightness of character – however laudable those might be – but through practical Christianity, faith demonstrated through action. What sort of action? The occasional good deed, kind word? Well, those might be a start, but, as the words of Jesus in the Sermon on the Mount make clear, he expects rather more than that. We are called to a love that goes beyond human expectations, confounding the way of the world. We are called, in other words, to a faith that *shows*.

Music *(optional)*

I give my work to you, Lord (Awakening in Love) Margaret Rizza

Reading

Matthew 5:38-48

Meditation of Matthew

Even tax-collectors!
What did he mean?
Was he having a dig at me or something?
For a moment I really thought so,
until he caught my eye and winked,
and I realised then it wasn't *me* he was teasing
but the crowd.
They thought they were so much better than I was,
chalk and cheese,
but he soon put them right,
showing that, at heart, we're all much the same.
We struggle to love, every one of us,
even what we feel for our nearest and dearest being flawed,
as much about *us* as anyone else.
That's the problem:
self gets in the way,
giving for what it can get,
expecting a *quid pro quo*,
and when that doesn't happen
our good intentions vanish on the breeze.
As for loving *others*,
those we don't get on with or who wish us ill:
forget it.
Yet that's what Jesus asked for,
and that's what he *did*:
loving people like me,
so-called tax-collectors and sinners;
loving *all*,
even those who nailed him to a cross;
loving both friends and enemies,
without reserve.
It was a hard way,
a costly way,
but it's the way that brought us life.
Lord, help me to love.

Quiet reflection

Prayer

Lord,
we *want* to love,
we *mean* to love,
we *try* to love,
but so often we fall short,
struggling to care for anyone but ourselves
and those closest to us.
Our fine intentions are sabotaged by greed,
pride,
envy,
resentment,
fear
and prejudice,
so that, time and again, we're found wanting.
Forgive us,
and help us to be channels of your love in Christ,
poured out so freely,
with no thought of the cost.
Flow in us,
and through us,
by his grace.
Amen.

Silence

Comment

Agreed, you might say, discipleship should show itself in action. But it's not the end of the world if it doesn't, for, after all, we depend on faith, not works; on the grace of God rather than any merit on our part. As far as it goes, that's true, none of us being able to earn our salvation, but it's a flawed argument nonetheless, for there's a fine line between acknowledging our dependence on God's mercy and becoming blasé about commitment, imagining that the way we live doesn't really matter.

Music *(optional)*

Let life rhythms flow (Sacred Pathway) Keith Duke

Reading

Matthew 7:21-29

Meditation of a would-be follower of Jesus

I've done what he asks, haven't I?
I've listened to his words,
considered his teaching.
And yes, he's right:
everything he says is spot on.
He's sent by God, no doubt about it:
the Messiah,
Lord,
Saviour of the world.
I acknowledge it all,
confess without reserve that he deserves our praise
more than any other.
That's enough, isn't it –
sufficient a response to ensure,
when the wind blows,
the rain falls
and the floods come,
that I stand firm,
secure in the fiercest storm?
What's that?
Something missing?
Deeds as well as words?
You mean faith is not enough?
That's a pity,
for it would make things so much easier.

'No need to send them away,' he said.
'*You* feed them!'
Well, we were flabbergasted.
I mean, how could anyone rustle up a meal out there
in the middle of nowhere?
We might have coped with the twelve of us, perhaps,
but there were masses to feed,
I'd say five thousand, at least.
We genuinely thought he was joking at first,
but he wasn't,
so we turned to the multitude and appealed for help,
and somehow,
despite there being only a few loaves and fish between them,
the food materialised –
not just a few scraps,
but enough to feed us all
with basketfuls left over.
It taught us a lesson that day about what God can do
if only we have faith,
but it taught us also about what *we* can do
when we're ready and willing to share.
If everyone walked the way of Christ,
putting others first and self second,
we could feed the needy again,
today, tomorrow and the next day,
for there's plenty to go round,
sufficient for all our needs and beyond.
We can't just leave it to God though –
that's not the way things work.
In a world where people still go hungry,
Jesus continues to bring that simple but scary challenge:
'*You* feed them!'

Quiet reflection

Prayer

God of all,
we wonder sometimes why you allow hardship to persist –
why you permit so many lives to be scarred by hunger,
disease,
poverty
and pain –
but though the question is real enough,
too often we forget that the answer lies in part with *us* –
so much misery being possible to avoid or relieve
if only we have sufficient will to work for change.
Teach us that you long to bring comfort, hope and justice
to those who cry out in need,
and help us to play our part in that ministry,
refusing to leave to you what we are able to do ourselves.
Amen.

Silence

Comment

What might God ask of me? Will I be able to rise to the challenge? How will I cope? For some, the idea that faith calls for action is a daunting one, for they fear God will ask from them more than they can give. And yes, undoubtedly there will be times when genuine commitment proves demanding, even stretching us to the limit. Yet for most of us, most of the time, commitment is not so challenging. It calls for action certainly, and yes, that may be costly in its way, but it's about playing to our strengths, consecrating who and what we are to God.

Music *(optional)*

Take my life and let it be (Traditional hymn) Frances Havergal

Reading

Matthew 25:14-30

Meditation of a reader of Matthew 25

I'll use my talents all right, don't you worry about that!
Well, you have to, don't you,
if you're to get on in this world?
And, like any other, I mean to do just that.
You know what they say,
'God helps those who help themselves',
so spot on, Jesus:
nice parable.
What's that you say?
I've got him wrong?
In what way?
You mean it's about serving *God*,
not self?
About using our gifts for *his* glory,
his kingdom,
rather than personal gain?
I'm not sure I like the sound of that,
though, now you mention it,
I guess it does fit rather better with the man and the message,
all that stuff of his about good news for the poor,
riches on earth,
treasure in heaven.
Shame, I was quite hopeful there,
thought I had *carte blanche* to feather my nest,
but it seems not,
the day coming when I'll be called to account.
Oh well, I must overcome the habit of a lifetime, I suppose,
learn to give rather than take,
but it won't be easy –
not without help.
Ah, *you* feel the same.
That's encouraging.

At least I'm not alone.
'In more ways than one!' you say?
'Not one of us left to cope on our own'?
Tell me more.

Quiet reflection

Prayer

'God helps those who help themselves' –
that's what people sometimes tell us, Lord,
and that's what we'd sometimes like the words of Jesus to mean,
for it makes them more comfortable to live with,
fitting in nicely with our instinctive approach to life.
Yet, deep down, we know that the gospel message
is not about doing well for ourselves,
looking after number one,
but about employing our gifts in whatever ways we can
to help further the growth of your kingdom.
Help us to do that,
consecrating our lives to your service.
Teach us to seek *your* glory and advancement
rather than our own.
Amen.

Silent retreat

Closing comment

Faith, we've been told, needs to show. So where does that leave us? Do we resolve to try harder? Do we make a list of the things we could and should be doing, and then attempt to tick them off one by one? We could try measures like those, but we probably wouldn't get very far, for we'd be back trying to do things again in our strength, faith becoming a matter of duty rather than joy. Certainly, a desire to follow more faithfully never comes amiss, but success in such a venture comes from God, not from us. We need his grace, his guidance, his help, his strength, and those come through opening our lives to his love and to the work of his Spirit within us. We have nothing to put into action unless God first gives us faith. And whether that shows depends on whether or not we remain one with him.

Closing prayer

Loving God,
we want to serve you,
mean to serve you,
but all too often our words say one thing,
our deeds another.
For all our talk of costly commitment,
the faith we profess rarely shows itself in the way we live,
if anything our lifestyles running contrary to the spirit of the gospel.
Help us to practise what we preach,
to put what we believe into action.
Give us a faith that makes a difference to who and what we are,
our love for you shaping everything we think and say and do.
Amen.

Responding to the call

Suggested visual material

Jesus of Nazareth 2
The Life of Christ II

FIRST SESSION

Introduction

The call of Christ: we use the phrase so often, so glibly, but what does it actually mean? Have we heard that call? Have we understood it? And, most important of all, have we responded? Today, through the words of Scripture, through reflections upon them, through prayer and through silence, we're going to reflect on that call and how it applies to our lives. We come asking Christ to speak again: eager to hear, eager to listen.

Opening prayer

Almighty God,
we remember how you called Abraham
to venture out into the unknown,
how you called Moses to lead your people out of Egypt,
how you called Elijah through a still small voice,
how you called prophets to speak your word,
how you called the disciples to follow Jesus,
how you called Saul on the Damascus Road,
and how you have called generations since, across the centuries,
to faith and service.
Through worship,
prayer,
Scripture
and daily life,

you have spoken your word,
summoning people to hear and answer.
Help us to listen to your voice in turn,
and to consecrate our lives to you in grateful response.
Amen.

Comment

There are times, aren't there, when it's wise to sit on the fence? Our partner asks what we think of their new suit or dress, and rather than hurt their feelings we mumble some noncommittal reply. We're asked by friends to arbitrate in a disagreement, but rather than take sides we encourage them to reach a compromise. An investment offers attractive rewards but also high risk, so we hedge our bets, putting in only some of our savings, or opting for, as it were, a halfway house. Caution can be the wisest course of action, but equally it can be misplaced. Our partner buys that suit or dress and both we and they end up hating it. The argument we thought we'd patched over goes on festering beneath the surface, one day exploding into a truly damaging confrontation. Our investment yields dividends so healthy that, had we sunk all our money into that policy, it could have set us up for life.

Sometimes we need to decide, for or against, and so it is with the call of Christ. A fudged decision is no decision at all. There can be no dodging the issue, no perching on two stools: we must make up our minds for ourselves.

Music *(optional)*

Credo (Mass in C Minor) Mozart

Reading

Matthew 16:13-20

Meditation of Andrew

He asked two questions,
almost the same
and yet so very different.

We'd no problem with the first,
for it was about *others* –
what *they* thought,
who *they* said he was –
but then he paused,
looking us straight in the eye,
and put us firmly on the spot.
'What about you:
who do you say that I am?'
There was no escaping it after that,
no hiding behind others.
He wanted *our* answer,
our response,
each of *us* being forced to decide.
Would we have done so otherwise?
I don't know,
for while we'd followed Jesus for months,
marvelling at his deeds and drinking in his every word,
we still wanted proof he was the one we waited for,
the deliverer our nation so earnestly yearned to see.
We admired him,
loved him even,
but we wanted to be sure before committing ourselves,
certain beyond a shadow of doubt that he was the real thing,
the answer to our prayers.
So we might well have procrastinated for ever,
measuring our words before daring to speak,
had not Peter waded in as usual,
grasping the bull by the horns.
'You are the Messiah, the Son of the living God.'
And of course he was right,
we all see it now,
but it was Peter's faith,
his willingness to take the plunge,
that helped to open our eyes.
We'd held back,
wanting the last reservation dispelled,

and could so easily have missed the wonderful truth
staring us in the face:
that God was with us,
right by our side,
come at last to set us free.
I believe it now.
My mind's made up,
decision made.
What about you?

Quiet reflection

Prayer

You ask us, Jesus,
as you asked your disciples long ago
and have asked generations since,
to decide for ourselves who you are.
Help us to answer that question,
not hedging our bets, as we are inclined to do,
nor sidestepping the issue,
nor hiding behind the conclusions of others,
nor taking refuge in cliché and jargon,
but honestly coming to our own conclusions
about what you have done
and what you mean for us.
And, having made our response,
help us to recommit to it each day,
so that our faith may be ever fresh,
ever real.
Amen.

Silence

Comment

If you belong to a charitable organisation such as the National Trust, English Heritage, RSPB or the like, you're probably given two options when it comes to renewing your subscription. You can either pay whatever fee is asked for another year or you can stump up a considerably larger sum for the privilege of life membership. Which you plump for probably depends on your age, your income and how passionately you feel about the organisation in question. If you're young, comfortably off and totally committed to the cause then it makes good economic sense to pay the extra and become a life member. If not, it probably doesn't.

How about when it comes to being a Christian, belonging to Christ? Can we sign up for life membership there too? Certainly we're called to lifetime commitment, but can that ever involve simply a one-off transaction, professing our allegiance and then sitting back to reap the dividends? The fact is that faith can blow hot one day and cold the next. To stay fresh, meaningful, real, we must renew our commitment, not just each year but each moment. We may have responded once, but what about now?

Music *(optional)*

Enfold me in your love (Fire of Love) Margaret Rizza

Reading

Matthew 21:23-32

Meditation of the chief priest

What a cheek!
What a nerve!
To compare us to tax-collectors,
prostitutes,
and then to suggest that *we* come off worst –
disgraceful!

Doesn't he realise who we are:
chief priests,
elders,
guardians of the Law?
But he knows full well,
that's the trouble,
making it all the harder to swallow.
He actually thinks he has the right to stand there
and tell us what God thinks,
as though *he's* an authority on such things,
and *we're* not.
Never mind our years of study and hours of prayer,
our knowledge of the commandments and our religious zeal –
this nobody from Nazareth knows best, doesn't he!
I mean, come on, get real.
And as for his insinuation that we're long on words
but short on action;
that the dregs of this world
understand what it means
to respond to God in a way we've not even begun to grasp –
well, honestly, what nonsense!
It's people like him who spell trouble,
not just to us but to religion as a whole.
He's clever, I'll grant him that,
playing the crowd like the Baptist before him,
but he'll go the same way in time –
let's face it, such would-be messiahs always do.
Let him weave his stories if he wants to –
we'll have the last laugh in the end –
for I tell you what,
if he really knew God's will
he'd have to be like that character in his parable –
the Father's *son* –
and not even he could mean that . . .
surely!

Quiet reflection

Prayer

Father God,
we like to think we've responded to you,
that we've heard your call and committed ourselves to your service,
but that doesn't necessarily mean anything in terms of here and now.
Help us to understand that having pledged our allegiance once
doesn't mean we're still faithful today,
for even the best intentions can easily come to nothing.
Teach us to recommit our lives to you each day,
examining our discipleship and seeking to ensure that it is as real now
as when we first began our journey.
By your grace help us to finish what we've started,
and, if necessary, to start out again.
Amen.

Silent retreat

SECOND SESSION

Comment

'Read the small print,' we're often told, and it's wise advice, for it's all too easy to sign up for something without really grasping what's involved. In extreme cases that can have dire consequences, as, for example, when we find we've committed ourselves legally and financially far more deeply than we imagined.

What of Christian discipleship? We've considered the need to respond to Christ's call and to keep on responding, day after day, but what is it that we're called to? Have we understood what it entails? As the following words from the Gospel of Matthew remind us, genuine commitment involves journeying in faith, trusting in God's provision, and accepting his guidance. It means preferring his way to that of the world, accepting the possibility of truly costly commitment, reaching out in his name despite hostility and rejection on the part of many. Are we up for the challenge?

Music *(optional)*

I will tread the earth lightly (Sacred Pathway) Keith Duke

Reading

Matthew 9:35–10:23

Meditation of Matthew

'Take no coins in your belts,
no wallet for your journey,
no spare tunic, sandals or a staff.'
Could he be serious, I wondered?
Surely not!
But he *was* –
we were to travel in faith,
confident that somewhere, somehow,
our needs would be met.
Well, my heart sank, you can imagine –
to set off on a journey
not knowing where the next meal is coming from,
without a shekel to your name,
not to mention a change of clothing,
that takes some doing, believe me!
He was right, though, I came to see that later,
for it taught us not simply to live by faith,
important though that may be,
but to sort out our priorities
and to travel light.
You see, we couldn't have gone far with a load on our backs,
a sackful of provisions.
We had to be free,
unencumbered,
able to stride out wherever he might lead us –
and that's what we did,
not just then, but later,
going out in his name to proclaim his word.

Yet that's not the end of it,
for those words of his were aimed not simply at *us* but at *you*,
as much about *your* journey as any.
'Do not worry about what you will eat, drink, wear,' he had said,
'but seek first the kingdom of God and his righteousness
and you will receive all these as well.'
'Sell everything, and give to the poor;
then come, follow me.'
'Come to me all you who are tired of carrying heavy loads
and I will give you rest –
take my yoke on you and learn from me,
for my yoke is easy
and my burden is light.'
In other words, let go of everything that binds us to earth,
that weighs us down and holds us back:
the grasping for riches and clinging to possessions
that consumes not just so much of our time but *us* as well,
leaving us empty instead of full,
hungry instead of satisfied.
Focus instead on the things that matter,
the resources he provides,
the true essentials of life.
I'm not telling you what to take for *your* journey –
that's between you and him –
but don't confuse what you want with what you need,
what will see you through with what will hold you back,
or else, far from being ready to travel
you may find yourself fit to drop,
and with nothing and no one to pick you up.

Quiet reflection

Prayer

Forgive us, Lord,
for our hearts lie too much with the things of this world,
with material possessions and earthly goals.

Those bring us pleasure for a time,
but ultimately offer fleeting contentment rather than true satisfaction,
holding us captive rather than setting us free.
Though we try to pretend otherwise,
studiously avoiding the truth,
we cannot deny the inner emptiness that you alone can fill.
Help us, then, to seek, before all else,
your kingdom and righteousness –
to let go of whatever weighs us down,
so that we may run the race you have set before us,
faithfully,
to the very end.
Amen.

Silence

Comment

One thing we're all adept at is making excuses to avoid what we'd rather not do. 'I'd love to . . . but . . .' 'I really wish I could . . . only . . .' There's usually some way of wriggling off the hook before we get hauled in. So it is when it comes to one of the most fundamental aspects of the call of Christ: the injunction to share our faith. We can come up with a host of reasons not to do so, some of them perhaps perfectly valid, but, if we're honest, one of the main reasons we keep quiet is that we're embarrassed; afraid of making a fool of ourselves, of what others might think. And, quite simply, that will not do. Yes, there's a time and a place for proclaiming the gospel; yes, clumsy evangelism can do more harm than good; yes, people may very well get the wrong end of the stick about us and what we're trying to do; but in some way, somehow, whether through word or deed, we need to communicate our faith to others. We may not all be evangelists, but we all have something to share. Are we responsive to that call?

Music *(optional)*

On the breath of the wind (Sacred Pathway) Keith Duke

Reading

Matthew 13:1-9, 18-23

Meditation of James

Some on the path;
on rocky ground;
among thorns?
That's not how I'd sow seed if I were a farmer.
I'd do the job carefully,
preparing the ground first
and scattering as much seed as possible on fertile soil
to ensure a bumper yield.
Why waste it?
It's a hard enough job working the land,
so why not maximise the harvest?
Only, of course, with people it's different,
as Jesus understood.
You can sow the seed of his word as carefully as you like,
but there's no telling if they're ready to receive it,
no way of knowing if it will take root or shrivel up,
grow strong or be choked by temptation.
It can bear fruit in the most unlikely of folk,
while those from whom you expect much remain barren,
the whys and wherefores of success being hard to fathom.
So then, don't take it for granted that his word will bear fruit in you,
for you may be wrong,
and don't give up on anyone else,
assuming that they'll never respond,
for there, too, you may be equally misguided.
Sow the seed in others,
and with God's help nurture it in yourself –
then leave the harvest to him.

Quiet reflection

Prayer

Loving God,
we trumpet the importance of mission,
of witnessing to you and making known your goodness,
but so often such talk is only words,
contradicted by the feebleness of our actions.
We come up with all kinds of reasons why people will refuse to listen,
and we use those as an excuse to keep things to ourselves,
hiding our light under a bushel.
Intentionally or otherwise,
we limit the scope of what you can do to our own expectations,
judging prospects by a human benchmark
instead of taking into account your divine power.
Help us,
simply, honestly and faithfully,
to sow the seed of your word,
keeping faith that in even the most unpromising of ground,
you can bring forth a harvest.
Amen.

Silent retreat

Closing comment

There was a time when it was commonplace to speak of people having a calling – not just to ministry or missionary work, but to all kinds of vocational professions. Nowadays such language seems to be less used, but an expression that has become familiar coinage is that of being 'on call'. Doctors, fire-fighters, care workers and a host of others can be summoned at the press of a button, each primed for rapid response.

As Christians, likewise, we are on call, all of the time, for Christ is constantly issuing his summons: to listen, to receive, to serve, to share, to make known his name in word and deed. Do you still live in the light of that challenge? Are you ready to respond?

Closing prayer

Wherever we go, Lord,
whatever else we do,
help us to respond to your call –
honouring you in our thinking and feeling,
speaking and doing,
working and resting,
living and loving.
Help us to hear your voice
and to answer.
Amen.

Who are we to judge?

Suggested visual material

Jesus of Nazareth 4
The Life of Christ II
St Paul

FIRST SESSION

Introduction

Who are we to judge? We'll all have said that many times over the years, but we can be pretty sure that we've been guilty infinitely more times of doing just what we say we shouldn't: judging others. For some reason, we just can't help ourselves. And more disconcerting still, we often don't even realise we're doing it. We may, of course, be quite right in our assessment of somebody; equally, we may be totally wrong. So much of what makes people tick, what shapes their thoughts and actions, their true motives for doing things, is hidden from public view. Why *do* we judge? What's wrong with doing so? What does it say about *us*? What does it say about *others*? It's questions like those that we're going to think about today, exploring them from the perspective of the words and actions of Jesus – the one who tells us: 'Judge not, lest you be judged; the judgement you give is the judgement you will get.'

Opening prayer

Lord Jesus Christ, we praise you,
for though you of all people had the right to sit in judgement,
you refused to do so,
looking always to pardon rather than condemn,
to forgive, renew, restore.
Thank you that alongside the worst you see the best,
alongside the bad, the good,

and though we reject your way, still you seek to welcome us back,
repeatedly offering another chance.
Give us a similar generosity of spirit,
a willingness to look for the worth in others
and to see beyond their faults.
Amen.

Comment

What's wrong with judging others? The answer is repeatedly spelt out in the teaching of Jesus. When a crowd bayed for the blood of a woman caught in adultery, he challenged whoever was without sin to cast the first stone. Similarly, in the Sermon on the Mount he asked how any of us can presume to take the speck out of our neighbour's eye when we have a colossal log protruding from our own. In other words, none of us can claim the moral high ground, still less the authority to condemn others for their mistakes. We all fall short, all go astray, each deserving judgement and being wholly dependent on God's grace. We assent to that in theory, but sadly all too often deny it in practice, clinging to a misplaced sense of virtue. It is sobering to reflect on the fact that Jesus highlighted a tendency among religious people in particular to consider themselves righteous when, as the following confrontation between Jesus and the Pharisees makes all too clear, they are in fact merely *self*-righteous.

Music *(optional)*

Chant for instruments (*Light in our Darkness)* Margaret Rizza

Reading

Matthew 9:9-13, 18-26

Meditation of a tax-collector

You should have seen their faces!
Disgusted or what!
It just wasn't done, mixing with low life like us,

and for a prophet, teacher or whatever he was,
it was unthinkable.
Yet he had no qualms,
no hesitation,
welcoming us with open arms.
I'm not saying he approved,
don't think that –
he no more condoned our faults than *they* did –
but he valued us as people,
his love not being conditional,
dependent on change,
but unreserved,
without strings.
He saw us as we were,
and loved us just the same,
giving us a sense of new beginnings,
a fresh start.
With him you felt that was actually possible –
indeed happening already –
for he believed in us
as we believed in him.
The Pharisees were appalled,
and I can't say I blame them,
but here's the thing:
we saw our faults,
they didn't see theirs.
It's not that Jesus had time for *us* and not for them,
despite how it may sound.
The trouble is they weren't as righteous as they liked to imagine,
merely *self*-righteous,
and until they learnt the difference
they would never recognise their need,
let alone turn to Jesus and find it answered.

Quiet reflection

Prayer

Save us, Lord, from self-righteousness,
from faith in ourselves rather than you,
in our own convictions and assumptions
rather than your way of love.
Help us to recognise the faults in *our* lives
and the virtues in others' –
our weaknesses and *their* strengths –
and to understand that we *all* fall short,
everyone being dependent on your grace.
Remind us that it is not our place to judge or condemn,
the measure we give being the measure we will receive.
Teach us, then, to open our hearts to you
and to all.
Amen.

Silence

Comment

It's hard sometimes, reading the Gospels, not to feel sorry for the scribes and Pharisees, for though they frequently came into conflict with Jesus they were undoubtedly sincere. In terms of faithfulness in worship, zeal in prayer, strictness in observance of the commandments and devotion in studying the Scriptures they were second to none, and, misguided though it was, their outrage at the words and deeds of Jesus was real. They weren't putting it on, using it as some kind of smokescreen behind which they could hide from the challenge his message brought. They genuinely felt shocked by his apparent disregard for the Law and open association with 'sinners'. The problem was they'd become fixated on the letter of the Law rather than the spirit, with their interpretation rather than its true meaning. Unconsciously – indeed, with the best of intentions – they'd set themselves up as arbiters of God's will, in so doing rejecting whatever failed to conform to their own. Do we make the same mistake?

Music *(optional)*

Miserere Gesualdo

Reading

Matthew 15:10-28

Meditation of a Pharisee

He was having a go again,
and we were incensed,
disgusted,
for he was undermining not just us
but the Law and the prophets –
the very fabric of our faith.
Take away our commandments,
our rituals refined over the years,
and where will we be then, I ask you?
Like everyone else, that's where:
no different from the common herd,
as unclean and unworthy as any.
So what was he thinking of,
contradicting our customs like that,
rewriting our rules,
as if he could see into the heart
and judge between good and bad,
right and wrong?
Instead of questioning what came out of *our* mouth
he should have looked to his own,
for his teaching was madness,
heresy,
leaving even his own disciples concerned.
Yet if *they* could see where his words were leading,
apparently *he* couldn't,
for, when some Canaanite woman turned up seeking his help,
he applauded her faith,
as though a Gentile,

a heathen,
could teach *us* of God;
as though all it takes to earn his favour
is to express trust and admit need!
He can't mean that, of course,
for it would open the door to all and sundry,
to anyone and everyone becoming his people,
and surely not even Jesus would go that far . . .
would he?

Quiet reflection

Prayer

Teach us, Lord, that it was not just those in centuries past
who presumed they could neatly package your will
into laws and commands;
that it is not simply others who make the mistake of thinking
that the essentials of faith can be reduced to rules and regulations.
Help us to see that, in our own way, we all do it,
attempting to fit you into neat categories that say more about *us*
than about *you*.
Open our minds to wider horizons,
viewpoints at variance with our own,
through which you are able to speak, challenge and guide.
Above all, open our hearts to *you*
and to the many ways you choose to work,
so often far exceeding our expectation or imagining.
Amen.

Silent retreat

SECOND SESSION

Comment

Intentionally or otherwise, we all judge others. We simply can't resist the urge. But we can't leave it there, for, as we have seen, Jesus firmly counselled against this innate yet hugely destructive human tendency. So how can we combat the urge to point the accusing finger? The answer is simple enough, at least to understand if not to act upon. We must learn to forgive, to cultivate the generosity of Christ in reaching out in love and acceptance. Why? Because he's shown such acceptance to us. How? Through opening our lives to the presence of his Spirit, so that he might transform from within. As the following experience of Simon Peter reminds us, it's not an easy lesson to learn, but if we're serious about discipleship it's one we should never forget.

Music *(optional)*

Mysterium amoris (Awakening in Love) Margaret Rizza

Reading

Matthew 18:21-35

Meditation of Simon Peter

Do you find forgiving easy?
I don't.
Oh, it's simple enough to say the words –
'apologies accepted' and all that –
but to *mean* them,
to pardon from the heart,
that's a different matter.
We can try, of course,
genuinely strive to let sleeping dogs lie,
but when you've been hurt, wronged, misjudged, mistreated,
it's hard to put that behind you,
as though it had never been.

Once, perhaps,
twice, maybe,
even a third time for some,
but as many as *seven* times?
I don't think so.
For most of us, by that point, trust is broken,
fractured beyond repair.
So when Jesus answered that question of mine,
suggesting not seven but *seventy-seven,*
you could have knocked me over,
such patience surely too much to ask of anyone!
Only it wasn't,
for he showed just that to *me,*
as he shows it *you,*
as he shows it to *all,*
daily forgiving and forgetting,
the ledger cleared,
the slate wiped clean.
There's no ceiling to his love,
no limit to his grace.
So next time you struggle to forgive,
just ask yourself this:
can't you pardon a little
for him who pardons so much?

Quiet reflection

Prayer

Merciful God,
we *intend* to forgive others,
we *try* to forgive others,
and we truly believe we *have* forgiven them,
but we find it so hard to let go of hurts,
grievances,
anger,
resentment.

Though we accept people's apologies
and try to put the past behind us
we find it almost impossible to let bygones be bygones,
the memory of wrongs done to us,
real or imagined,
festering within,
welling up to the surface at a moment's notice.
Help us to be more like you,
able to forgive and forget.
Work within us,
and nurture a genuinely generous and merciful spirit.
Amen.

Silence

Comment

We know we shouldn't judge yet we still do so. We know we ought to forgive but we struggle to let go of hurts and resentment. The spirit is willing but the flesh is weak. If that's how you feel, don't despair, for you're not alone. Throughout the history of the Church, people have grappled with the same problem, and no doubt they always will. Early believers struggled to accept that Saul, their most feared persecutor, was suddenly one of their number, called by Christ to share in making him known. Christians in Jerusalem wrestled with the idea of Gentiles being admitted to their ranks without having to observe the requirements of the Law. Arguments raged over gifts of the Spirit, the eating of food previously offered to idols, and correct practice in the Lord's Supper. And in centuries since, Catholics have condemned Protestants and Protestants Catholics as just one instance of divisions that have racked Christendom. Time and again, God's people have forgotten the all-important truth that judgement is in God's hands, not ours. Who are we to question where and when he shows his generosity?

Music *(optional)*

Qui tollis peccata mundi (Gloria) Vivaldi

Reading

Matthew 20:1-16

Meditation of the Apostle Paul

Were they jealous of me, my fellow apostles?
Yes, they probably were at first,
and on a human level, who can blame them?
For they'd walked and talked with Jesus
before I'd even heard the name;
working for his kingdom while I did my best to destroy it.
I was a latecomer,
an upstart,
in every sense the least of their number,
yet Jesus called me to faith and service,
an inheritance among the saints.
I didn't deserve it,
not in the slightest,
nothing I said or did earning his favour.
It was grace, pure and simple,
his love poured out,
generous to a fault.
But then that's true for us all, isn't it,
each of us saved through faith, not works,
through what God has done for *us* rather than us for *him*?
We forget that fact too often,
turning the gospel into carrot and stick,
obedience and reward,
a bargain in which, if we keep our side, God must keep his.
Only there's no gospel there,
no message of hope –
quite the opposite,
for we'll get nowhere on merit,
our just deserts to be feared, not welcomed.
So don't fret about God's dealings with others,
whether he's as fair as you'd like him to be:
that's *his* business, no one else's.
Remember he's dealt kindly with you,

more than you've any right to expect,
and let that be more than enough.

Quiet reflection

Prayer

Though we talk about your grace, Lord,
your free and undeserved pardon,
we don't really believe in it –
not if we're honest.
We're drawn, instinctively, to the creed of an eye for an eye
and a tooth for a tooth,
or at least to the modern-day equivalent:
that punishment should fit the crime.
The idea of wrongdoing being pardoned,
a sentence quashed,
goes against the grain,
contradicting our idea of natural justice,
and, for the stability of society and good of all,
we know we need laws to be fairly but firmly enforced.
Yet we forget that, in relation to you, we all fall short,
none of us being blameless,
still less meriting your love and mercy.
Forgive our temerity in being swift to condemn,
slow to pardon,
and help us to leave judgement where it belongs:
with you.
Amen.

Silent retreat

Closing comment

We've all cast judgement where we shouldn't have done, and no doubt will do so again in the future. We can't change ourselves overnight, however much we'd like to. But what we *can* do is think about the judgements we've made and continue to make, and ask what lies behind them. Think for a moment of the people you've condemned with barely a second thought. Consider the attitudes you've held and the assumptions that have shaped them, the prejudices that lurk deep within. And ask how you would fare were Christ to judge you in the same way. Pause, ponder and, where necessary, seek his help to change.

Closing prayer

As we return to our daily lives, Lord,
give us realism in all our dealings with others,
but also wisdom, compassion and understanding.
Help us to make allowances where appropriate;
to see the other's points of view.
Above all, help us to recognise our weakness,
our mistakes,
and so to avoid casting the first stone
when it could so easily be hurled at us,
but for your saving grace.
Amen.

On earth as it is in heaven

Suggested visual material

The Parables of Jesus

FIRST SESSION

Introduction

'Your kingdom come, on earth as it is in heaven' – so run the words of the Lord's Prayer, and we repeat them week after week with barely a second thought. But do we mean what we say? Do we in fact have any sense whatsoever of God's kingdom growing around us? Most of us, if we think of the kingdom at all, probably consign it to the distant future, end times, seeing it as synonymous with heaven, belonging to an altogether different dimension from anything we experience now. That might be what *we* mean, but it's certainly not what Jesus had in mind. The kingdom of God has come, he declared at the start of his ministry. It is here among you, to be found within. Yes, its consummation lies in the future. Yes, we glimpse it but in part, what we see in this life being only a portent of things to come. But it's real nonetheless, God here and now, despite all that conspires against him, seeking to work out his purpose in human lives. Today we pause to consider what that means, and to commit ourselves afresh to the kingdom's growth among us.

Opening prayer

Gracious God,
we thank you for the hope you have given us in Christ,
the promise of your eternal kingdom
in which there will be no more pain, sorrow, evil or death.
We thank you that we can look beyond this life to a life to come,
beyond this world to a new heaven and earth,

in which your will shall finally be done.
But we thank you also for life now,
and the fact that you are present within it;
for the joy, loveliness and blessings that surround us –
so much to thrill and satisfy
despite everything that conspires against your love.
Teach us that you have not washed your hands of this world,
but instead loved it enough to die for it;
that you care about the welfare of all
and seek to guide, protect, renew and restore.
Help us to glimpse your presence among us,
to recognise your hand at work,
and, through offering our service,
to play our part in bringing your kingdom closer here on earth,
even as it is in heaven.
Amen.

Comment

For many, any suggestion that the kingdom of heaven is present among us now is simply ridiculous. How can we begin to talk in such terms when our world is racked by evil, injustice, tragedy and disaster on every side? No, they say, this world is irredeemably lost, and we must pin our hopes entirely on life to come. There's no denying that such a counsel of despair is, at times, understandable, but it runs contrary to the message of Christ. He was well aware, of course, of everything that's wrong with our world, seeming to thwart and deny God's purpose, but he spoke despite that of the seeds of his kingdom being sown among us. And the following parable perhaps helps just a little in helping us to come to terms with the bad that God allows to scar the good, the sorrow that mars the joy. For now, those must exist side by side. There is no other way.

Music *(optional)*

Have mercy, Lord (St Matthew Passion) J. S. Bach

Reading

Matthew 13:24-30, 36-43

Meditation of a listener to Jesus

He spoke of separating wheat from weeds,
of harvesting the one and discarding the other,
as though the two can be clearly distinguished.
And, of course, they *can*,
but what about good and evil,
right and wrong –
the dichotomy Jesus really had in mind –
are they so easily disentangled?
Oh, there's a difference all right,
all the difference in the world,
but which best describes you?
Isn't there a bit of both in each of us?
There is in *me*, that's for sure,
worthy deeds one minute being marred by unworthy ones the next.
So, when the time for judgement comes,
where will that leave us:
considered fruitful,
fit to be saved,
or cast aside like so much chaff?
It's not straightforward is it?
And perhaps Jesus never meant it to be,
his precise point being that, in all of us, good and evil grow together –
that alongside the fertile seed he sows in our hearts
there is that sown by temptation,
both competing for a hold.
That's the way of things in this life,
the way it's always been,
but one day, he tells us, it will change,
his kingdom seeing an end to all that opposes his will.
Until then, we must cultivate the good as best we can,
thankful for his mercy now
and trusting in his grace to come.

Quiet reflection

Prayer

Merciful God,
we mean to serve you,
but so often go astray;
we intend to do good,
but end up doing evil;
we strive to walk the way of Christ,
yet repeatedly follow our own inclinations.
Take the germ of faith within us,
the seeds of genuine commitment,
and nurture them through your love
so that they may grow strong and vigorous,
despite everything that competes against them.
Grant that, through your grace,
any weeds that have crept into our lives
may be far outweighed by a bumper crop –
a rich and healthy harvest speaking of you.
Amen.

Silence

Comment

'From little acorns spring mighty oaks'; 'Drop by drop fills the bucket'; 'The beginnings of all things are small' – just some of the countless proverbs that take as their theme the fact that unexpected results can stem from the smallest of starts. What seems incapable of having any impact whatsoever can lead to altogether disproportionate results; a drop in the ocean, for example, sending out ripples far across the water. The same idea features in several of Jesus' parables concerning the kingdom of heaven. Tiny actions on our part, of themselves seemingly insignificant, can help it to take shape, God using them by grace in ways far exceeding our expectations. Just as seasoning adds flavour to a meal or yeast causes dough to rise, so our words and actions, offered in faith, can help to make a real and vital difference. You may feel there's little if anything you can contribute to furthering God's cause, but, as the following parables remind us, you'd be wrong.

Music *(optional)*

Inpoured Spirit (River of Peace) Margaret Rizza

Reading

Matthew 13:31-33, 44-52

Meditation of Martha, the sister of Mary

I could relate to that parable of his,
for I've made bread more times than I can remember,
and it's amazing the difference a little yeast makes to the loaf.
That,
and that alone,
causes it to rise.
I make *unleavened* bread as well, of course,
eaten at our Passover meal:
a reminder of how our people hurried from captivity
in search of the Promised Land –
no time for yeast,
no time for anything.
And it seemed to me that Jesus was drawing a comparison
between that kingdom and his,
for the kingdom of heaven is here among us,
taking shape day by day.
There's no rush to complete it,
to escape from this world.
It's a reality we must help to build,
serving as yeast to help it grow.
Yes, its fulfilment lies in another place and time,
but if we see it as only there
then we'll fail to see it all,

for it's also about love,
service,
commitment,
compassion,
offered here, today, on earth.
The old way is past,
the new has come,
his love has set us free.

Quiet reflection

Prayer

Sovereign God,
though we look forward to a new heaven and earth,
a kingdom that is yet to come,
save us from turning our back on the present,
as though the here and now is unimportant
and the world around us is not our concern.
Save us from washing our hands
of social and environmental responsibility;
of loving our neighbour, both near and far;
of working out our faith in daily life;
of testifying to your love through words and deed.
Teach us that if we would truly enter your kingdom
we must strive each day to bring it closer,
on earth as it is in heaven.
Amen.

Silent retreat

SECOND SESSION

Comment

We've spoken of the temptation to pin all our hopes for God's kingdom on some distant time in the future: another time, another place, another world. Isn't that exactly what the great vision of Revelation tells us to do, speaking of a new heaven and earth, a new Jerusalem unlike anything we can currently know or imagine? Isn't that at the heart of the Christian conception of the heavenly city God holds in store for us? Yes . . . and no. Certainly anything we can build or experience now is but a shadow of what's yet to come; a foretaste of the heavenly banquet in which one day we shall share, but that doesn't mean we can dismiss this world and our responsibilities within it, that we can live with our head in the clouds, looking forward longingly to end times when God's will at last is done. The teaching of Jesus emphatically makes that point, repeatedly warning against the dangers of speculating about the future, of dwelling on times, dates or anything else concerning the realisation of his purpose. Focus instead, he said, on the present, on helping to make God's kingdom real here and now. By all means be shaped by the hope of things to come, but translate it into action through faithful service and daily discipleship. Only if we help build that kingdom now will we recognise it when it finally and fully comes.

Music *(optional)*

Christ, be near (Sacred Pathway) Keith Duke

Reading

Matthew 24:1-14

Meditation of a first-century Christian

War!
Famine!
Persecution!

Earthquakes!
I don't much like the sound of this;
in fact, forgive me for saying so,
but if that's what it takes to establish God's kingdom,
I hope it never comes.
But hang on,
not so fast,
for haven't such things always been,
from the beginning of time?
Nations have squabbled, brawling like kids,
and disasters come and go –
always have,
always will.
We wish it were different,
but it's a fact of life,
nothing new.
Yes, some seize on every fresh trouble,
saying, 'There you are!
Isn't this what he said?
The end is at hand!'
But prophecies have come . . .
prophecies have gone . . .
raising people's hopes only to dash them again.
And now I look more closely,
isn't that what Jesus warned against:
speculating over times and dates,
as though we can know for sure when his kingdom will come?
Beware of any,
friend or foe,
who gives up on *this* world for the sake of the next.
Certainly, we must look to the kingdom,
anticipate its dawn,
but we must work to make it real,
here on earth as it is in heaven.
We must live *now*,
love *now*,
the future *shaping* rather than *taking over* the present,
for there's a world to be saved,

a world to be served,
and if faith forgets that then it's no faith at all.
This is the day the Lord has made,
not tomorrow.
In sunshine or shadow,
triumph or trial,
let us be glad in him . . .
until he comes.

Quiet reflection

Prayer

Remind us, Lord, that you call us not to speculate about the future,
about the date and time of your return,
but simply to trust that eternity is in your hands,
and to live each moment in the light of that assurance.
Teach us that the life you offer –
abundant and overflowing –
is not postponed to some distant future but starts now,
shaped, guided and sustained by your loving hand.
Help us, then, to rejoice and be glad,
living each day wisely and faithfully,
in sure and certain hope.
Amen.

Silence

Comment

Building the kingdom of heaven on earth: a daunting challenge undoubtedly, but also a wonderful thought. Does that mean, though, that we can push the future to one side, forgetting all about Christ's promise to come again? Does the here and now take precedence over the yet to be? The question is more apparent than real, for – as our next and final parable reminds us – the two are inseparable. Our hope lies ultimately and always in what God holds in store, but that hope should necessarily shape the present. We seek to build God's kingdom on earth as it is in heaven, which means we must live in such a way that we're ready at any moment for heaven to break in on earth.

Music *(optional)*

Sinfonia (Messiah) Handel

Reading

Matthew 25:1-13

Meditation of Mary, sister of Martha and Lazarus

His words struck a chord with me,
for, like those bridesmaids he spoke of,
I've been caught short all too often,
left with my lamp empty when it should have been full.
You know how it is:
the oil's running low,
but, no worries, you can deal with that later –
only it slips your mind until night comes,
leaving you stumbling around in darkness.
Could that happen with faith,
reserves exhausted there too?
You may not think so of *me*,
for wasn't *I* the one who sat at his feet,
drinking in his every word while Martha fussed and fretted?
Yet don't be fooled,
for kindling the flame is not enough.
It must be kept burning,
kept alive,
and that means feeding it day by day,
lest the fuel run dry.
And that can happen, you know –
to you,

to me,
to anyone –
distractions of this world causing faith to fail
as we put self first, God second,
time for *us* before time for *him*.
Take care,
stay alert,
keep watch,
so that, should your lamp go out,
you can light it again.

Quiet reflection

Prayer

Are we ready to meet you, Lord?
Prepared for your coming?
If you walked in upon us today,
tomorrow,
the next day,
would our lives measure up to your call,
or would we be embarrassed by your presence,
hastily making excuses to cover our shame
at our false and feeble discipleship?
Remind us that though you do not want us to fret about end times,
you *do* want us to be prepared for your coming,
the promise that you will come again shaping everything we think,
say and do.
In that knowledge,
may we consecrate every moment to you
as though it were our last.
Amen.

Silent retreat

Closing comment

Just as there are two sides to every coin, so there are two sides to God's kingdom. It's about the present but also the future, about what is now yet also what is yet to come. Both are part of the whole. We are called not simply to look forward to what God will do; rather we must play our part in helping it come to pass, sowing seeds of the kingdom through the service we offer, and the love and compassion we show. And, further, we must glimpse God's presence around us – through worship and fellowship, through one another and those we meet, through the world around us and the events of daily life. In one sense we are entrusted with helping to bring the kingdom closer on earth as it is in heaven. In another, we are called to recognise it is here already. That is the challenge and wonder of faith!

Closing prayer

Give us, Lord, a vision not just of your kingdom in heaven,
but also of your kingdom on earth,
a sense of what you want to do and are able to do,
here and now among us.
Give us love for you
and for others;
faith in you
and faith in them.
Grant a sense of your presence and power,
of your gracious will,
and may that inspire us each day to joyful service,
for your kingdom's sake.
Amen.

Come wind, come weather

Suggested visual material

Jesus of Nazareth 5
The Life of Christ II and III

FIRST SESSION

Introduction

Take a walk during the summer on Dartmoor, the Pennines, or the mountains of Wales and Scotland, and the chances are that you'll enjoy a relatively undemanding expedition. There'll be the occasional tough incline, of course, the odd stretch of boggy ground or rough track, and you may, if you've chosen unwisely, catch a downpour or two. But, by and large, you'll be left wondering why some people make such a fuss about the dangers and difficulties of walking in such hill country. Attempt the same trip in the winter, however, and it will very likely be a different story. Try walking on the fells, for example, in the teeth of a howling gale, or struggling up Snowdon as snow is falling and the chill eats into your bones, and you may well resolve never to go walking again. Most of us when it comes to the country-side are very much fair-weather aficionados. As long as the sun shines it's all very wonderful; otherwise, forget it.

The same can be true, though we may not like to admit it, of Christian discipleship. So long as allegiance involves joy, blessing, answers to prayer and so forth, you won't find more dedicated followers than us. But when it means costly commitment, or when we find ourselves up against trials and tribulations, our loyalty can wear thin, faith starting to fray at the edges, if not unravel altogether. Yet it is precisely at times like these that true faith shows its mettle, and at times like these also that we both need God and, if we hold fast, can find him. It's not that we revel in hardship or delight in persecution – far from it – but we believe God can use even the darkest moments of life in his purpose. Today, then, we reflect on what the words and deeds of Jesus say to us about faith in adversity; about how, through him, God is able to work together in all things for good.

Opening prayer

Loving God,
we remember how in the darkness of Gethsemane,
the grimness of the cross,
you were there,
strengthening your Son in his time of need,
assuring him that, through drinking the cup of suffering,
he would bring blessing to all.
We remember how, across the years,
people of faith have endured untold testing,
ready even to give their lives in turn for your sake.
Help us to recognise that you are with us just as much when life is bad
as when it is good;
that you are able to take what seems to deny your goodness
and contradict your love,
and to weave it into your gracious purpose.
Remind us that though in this world there is much
that frustrates your will,
all creation groaning as if in childbirth,
the day will come when sorrow and suffering will be at an end.
Teach us, then, when life is hard and days are demanding,
to keep faith,
trusting that you are able to see us through,
through Jesus Christ our Lord.
Amen.

Comment

The teaching of Christ, just like the idea of suffering being turned to good, can seem almost ludicrously counterintuitive, flying in the face of common sense. Nowhere is that more the case than in the so-called Beatitudes, where Jesus repeatedly turns the received wisdom of this world upside down, deeming as blessings what most people would consider to be a curse. Chief among those is surely the proposal that we should somehow welcome persecution. Is he really suggesting this might be a good thing in itself? Of course not. No one in their right minds would willingly court pain or hostility. Yet there are times when standing up for what we know to be right necessarily involves cost; a cost that many have been prepared to pay over the years. Why? Because they consider the cause for which they're suffering to be more than worth it. Because they believe it to be something bigger, greater than themselves. Because they believe they'd be unable to live with themselves were they to turn their back on principles and convictions they hold dear. None of us wants to be put in that position, but how would we respond if we were?

Music *(optional)*

Communion for All Saints' Day Anonymous

Reading

Matthew 5:1-12

Meditation of Simon Peter

I couldn't get it at first.
What blessing can there be in persecution,
in facing hatred and hostility for the sake of Christ?
All right, so they slandered the prophets before us,
hurling all kinds of insults against them,
but that doesn't make it good, does it,
let alone something to be desired?
Surely there must be easier ways to secure heaven's rewards,
a less costly and demanding path?
What about those other things he mentioned,
like hungering and thirsting after righteousness?
Won't one of them do instead?
Okay, so I'm not as meek and merciful as I should be,
as poor in spirit or pure in heart,
but I'm working on it

and will get there in the end.
But can any of those stand alone,
in splendid isolation from the rest?
There's the rub.
I want to say yes,
but his words said no,
everything he said and taught
speaking of distinctive commitment,
a way of life different from the world's,
challenging its norms and undermining the status quo.
In other words, true faith will ruffle feathers,
get under people's skin,
and that spells trouble,
for they won't like it –
won't like it at all,
and they'll silence us if they can,
just as they tried to silence him.
It's easier to keep your head down,
to conform with the crowd and not ask awkward questions,
but from this challenge, at least, there's no running away.
I can stay in my comfort zone and leave others in theirs,
or I can stay true to Christ.
Sadly I can't do both.

Quiet reflection

Prayer

Living God,
give us, where necessary, the courage to be different,
to go against the expectations of the world
when they conflict with your truth, your way, your will.
Help us, as far as possible, to live peaceably with all,
never seeking confrontation or discord,
but aware also that there will be times when,
like those who have gone before us,
we must make a stand,
sticking up for the things we believe in,
even though that may entail scorn,

hostility,
rejection.
Inspire us through the life and witness of saints of old –
their faith, service and commitment –
to walk in their footsteps.
Save us from loving the world so much that we love you less,
from confusing the rewards of earth with the joys of heaven –
blessings you alone can give.
Amen.

Silence

Comment

There are no easy answers to why God allows suffering, why our world is scarred by pain, hatred and evil, but, as our first reading and meditation reminded us, there is one form of hardship that we can make sense of, and that is when it comes as a result of faithfulness to the call of Christ. Walking the way of love, the path of Christian discipleship, may well involve some kind of sacrifice. For some, of course, it's truer than for others: those, for example, who live in parts of the world where they face repression and persecution for holding fast to their convictions. Much less is asked of *us*, yet commitment can still prove costly. What does the experience of Jesus and his first disciples say to us today?

Music *(optional)*

Prayer for peace (River of Peace) Margaret Rizza

Reading

Matthew 6:25-34

Meditation of Simon Peter

'Don't worry about tomorrow,' he said,
and I could relate to that,
for I'm an impulsive kind of guy,

jumping in with both feet, never mind the consequences.
Act now, think later, that's my motto,
and by and large it's served me well,
for if I'd fretted about the whys and wherefores of my decisions
I'd have missed half the experiences that have made me what I am.
His words make sense too,
for worry doesn't change things, does it? –
only makes them worse.
You can brood all you like,
but it won't make you live one whit longer –
more likely the opposite.
It's hard work that puts food on the table and clothes on your back;
no more, no less.
So yes, I understood where he was coming from
and warmed to his message –
after all, with him by our side, what could we possibly have to fear?
Only that was then,
before events panned out the way they did,
before they nailed him to a cross and laid him in a tomb,
my friend and master done to death.
If I'd known earlier what was coming I'd have worried all right,
but though he'd often talked of suffering and sacrifice,
I never seriously believed he meant it –
always felt it must be some kind of figure of speech,
a way of emphasising the point.
It wasn't of course –
he was in deadly earnest –
and the extraordinary thing is that he knew all along
where his ministry would lead,
that he was born to die . . .
yet still he told us not to worry.
How could he do that?
What on earth could he mean?
But that's just it,
he wasn't thinking of earth so much as of heaven,
of blessing beyond this world.
We're not exempt from life's trials –
not you,

not me,
not anyone –
but whatever the future may hold, our destiny is assured.
Keep faith, he said,
keep trusting,
for his love will see you through.
Though much may touch the body
it can never harm the soul.

Quiet reflection

Prayer

Father God,
you tell us not to worry,
but we find it hard not to,
for there is so much in life that *can* go wrong
and so much that *does*.
We fret about the safety of loved ones;
about keeping our job, paying the bills;
about our health and the prospect of growing old;
about the state of the world –
all this and so much more –
for we know that faith offers no exemption from trouble,
our trials being as tough and challenging as anyone's.
Help us to keep that sense of realism,
but also to remember that you promise us strength in times of need,
peace in moments of turmoil
and comfort in times of grief –
above all, a life and a world to come
in which suffering and sorrow will be no more,
and your love will be all in all.
In that hope we put our trust.
Amen.

Silent retreat

SECOND SESSION

Comment

Suffering for the cause of Christ: it may not be welcome, but at least it's understandable. What of the traumas and tragedies that afflict us as part of daily life, seemingly without any rhyme or reason – how do we cope with those? Does faith have anything meaningful to offer that will help to see us through? That's what we're going to consider in this session, and we start with perhaps some of the best-loved and most familiar of all Jesus' words: his invitation to those tired of carrying heavy loads to find rest in him. Help in time of need: that's what faith should mean, but we can unconsciously twist it sometimes out of all recognition. Does faith relieve our burdens, or add to them?

Music *(optional)*

In God alone is my soul at rest (In God Alone) Andrew Moore

Reading

Matthew 11:16-19, 25-30

Meditation of Matthew

Are *you* weary,
tired of carrying a heavy load?
I was, though I didn't know it at the time,
didn't quite grasp what it was that warmed me to Jesus
when he found me at the tax-collector's booth and asked me to follow.
I obeyed without a second thought,
in the blink of an eye turning from one life to another,
and if you'd have pressed me for my reasons
I'd probably have said it was curiosity or a thirst for adventure –
nothing deeper than that.
But I'd have been wrong,
for the truth is I was worn out,
if not in mind and body then in spirit.

I'd not yet admitted it to myself,
but life was a relentless quest for gain,
to feather my nest as best I could,
so I'd swindled and extorted in the name of Rome,
selling out, not just my countrymen,
but my very soul.
Yes, I made light of it,
wearing a careless smile for the world,
but the shame and emptiness within hung heavy upon me –
a manacle from which I could not break free.
Until, that is, I met Jesus,
and found new life,
new beginnings –
the past put aside,
mistakes forgiven:
rest for my soul.
The chains *you* wear may be altogether different,
but the answer's the same, take it from me,
for I've followed Jesus these last few years
and seen so many set free.
Whatever your burden,
stop wrestling with it on your own.
Give it to him –
give *everything* to him, yourself included –
and let go.

Quiet reflection

Prayer

How do we do it, Lord?
How do we turn a message of deliverance
into a religion that enslaves,
a gospel of freedom into a travesty of faith
that remorselessly holds us captive?
It shouldn't be possible,
but we do it time and again,

adding to the trials of life by weighing ourselves down with guilt,
rules,
demands
and expectations –
each of our own making rather than yours.
Remind us that your yoke is easy and your burden light;
that you invite us to cast whatever loads we carry
on to your shoulders,
confident that you are strong enough to bear not just them
but us too.
Help us, then, truly to let go,
and to find rest in body, mind and soul.
Amen.

Silence

Comment

One of the best-loved visual images of Jesus is that of him commanding the waves, calming the sea and stilling the storm, delivering his disciples from the wild unpredictability of the elements. Generations have applied this incident to their own lives, experiencing moments where they felt not only all at sea but as though they were going under, overwhelmed by the storms of life. The analogy was employed centuries earlier by the writer of Psalm 69: 'Save me, O God, for the waters have come up to my neck. I sink in a deep mire, where there is no foothold; I have come into deep waters, and the flood sweeps over me' (vv. 1, 2). Always, though, the testimony of Scripture is the same: God is faithful, able to calm not only the wildest of storms but also the turmoil in our lives. Problems may still continue, suffering and sorrow may still be real, and we may still struggle to make sense of our experience, but he will see us safely through.

Music *(optional)*

You are my refuge (Sacred Weave) Keith Duke

Reading

Matthew 14:22-33

Meditation of Simon Peter

The wind was against us that day,
blowing us ever further from land,
and the waves rose by the minute,
battering our little boat like so much flotsam.
We weren't landlubbers remember –
we were used to such conditions –
but we were nervous just the same,
feeling lost and alone on the hostile sea . . .
until suddenly Jesus appeared,
walking on the water towards us,
hands outstretched in welcome.
Extraordinary!
I responded instinctively,
stepping out of the boat to meet him.
Only suddenly the reality of what I'd done hit me,
and if Jesus hadn't reached out and caught hold,
I'd have sunk like a stone.
That's true for us all, in a way,
for in life, as at sea, the wind can be equally against us.
We face troubles to test the strongest,
and, on our own –
battered by trials and tribulations –
we'd surely go under,
unable to keep afloat.
But, of course, we're *not* alone,
for Jesus is always there through his Spirit,
to help and strengthen in time of need.
Just as he made me feel I could walk on water,
so each day he does similarly for others:
instilling faith,
inspiring hope,
imbuing trust.

Don't look at the problems you're up against,
the sea of doubt, difficulty and despair.
Look to him . . .
and walk tall.
His love will not fail.

Quiet reflection

Prayer

Loving God,
when we're up against problems,
up to our neck in difficulties that threaten to sweep us away,
teach us never to despair.
Remind us that, with your help,
we can do more than we might first believe,
your strength able to make up for our weakness.
Teach us, then,
whatever we may face,
however daunting the obstacles before us,
to trust in you,
confident that your power is able to see us through.
Amen.

Silent retreat

Closing comment

Walking the way of Christ is not, as we might first imagine, a gentle jog, casual stroll. It's certainly not a walk in the park in which everything is guaranteed to go smoothly. It's a marathon, calling for perseverance, a lifetime commitment during which we'll inevitably have to face bad times as well as good, tears as well as laughter. If anything, it's likely to prove more demanding than the way of the world. But it's not a way we walk alone, for in the journey of discipleship Christ, through his Spirit, is there by our side. Attempt to get by on our own and we will stumble and fall, unable to stay the course. Put our trust in him, stay close, and we will stand firm to the end – come wind, come weather.

Closing prayer

Help us to walk with you, Lord,
whatever the journey of faith may bring.
In times of testing, give strength.
In times of despair, give hope.
In times of sorrow, give comfort.
In times of hurt, give healing.
Teach us that however demanding the road may seem,
you will be with us on it,
every step of the way,
and in that faith may we match our stride to yours.
Amen.

A living hope

Suggested visual material

Jesus of Nazareth 4–6
The Life of Christ II and IV

FIRST SESSION

Introduction

We are those, says the first letter of Peter (1:3), born by the mercy of God into a living hope through the resurrection of Jesus Christ from the dead; in other words, those whose ultimate destiny lies not in this world but in a new heaven and earth to come. We look forward, as Christians, to a kingdom in which sorrow and suffering will be no more, in which we will see and know God face to face, in which his will shall finally and fully be done. But is hope, then, consigned to the distant future? What, if anything, does faith have to say about the present? In what way is the kingdom of God here among us now? Furthermore, how far can we talk meaningfully of life beyond this world? Is it possible to envisage what that means or are we left constantly clutching at straws? It's questions such as these that we're going to ponder today, not expecting easy answers but through readings, reflections, silence and prayer seeking guidance and understanding, a deeper faith and greater awareness of God's eternal purpose.

Opening prayer

Almighty God,
we have drawn aside from the world
so that we might return to it with faith renewed.
We have set this time apart
so that we might consecrate time itself,
offering our past, present and future to you.

We have come to be silent so that we might hear,
to empty ourselves so that we might be filled,
to make some space in our busy schedules
so that you may find room in our hearts
to teach, challenge, inspire and nurture.
Meet with us now,
and help us to meet with you,
through Jesus Christ our Lord.
Amen.

Comment

We start today by focusing specifically on what Jesus himself had to say concerning God's promise of eternal life, and we start where the journey of so many comes to an abrupt end: with the leap of faith needed to believe in the reality of resurrection and the presence of the living Christ. Where does that begin and on what is it based? Our first reading and meditation set the scene.

Music *(optional)*

Lift up your heads O ye gates (Messiah) Handel

Reading

John 10:22-30

Meditation of a Sadducee listening to Jesus

Why didn't he tell us who he was?
Why beat about the bush,
talking in parables and riddles,
when he could have made things clear?
Was he the Messiah or wasn't he?
But he wouldn't come clean,
seeming determined instead to keep us guessing.

Well, what could we make of that?
It seemed obvious he wasn't the Messiah after all,
but that he wanted us to think he *might* be;
that, despite all his claims to the contrary,
he enjoyed the mystique,
the attentions of the crowd,
and wanted to keep it going.
Even then, though, we wanted to believe,
hoping we might be wrong,
so we put him on the spot,
asking him to give it to us straight,
one way or the other.
And what did he talk about in reply?
Sheep!
I know: extraordinary, isn't it!
He seemed to imply we had only to listen
and the truth would be revealed,
but that we'd made up our minds already
and were resolved *not* to hear.
What nonsense!
The truth is that, for all his signs and wonders,
God's reign on earth seemed as far away as ever,
consigned to some future kingdom
rather than established here today.
Well I'm sorry, but we don't go in for all that pie-in-the-sky nonsense –
resurrection and eternal life –
and we never will
unless someone comes back from the dead to prove it.
Let Jesus do that and we'll revise our opinion,
of him and everything,
for *of course* we'd believe then –
who wouldn't? –
but I don't think that's likely.
Do *you*?

Quiet reflection

Prayer

Living Lord,
in a sceptical and cynical world that refuses to believe,
help us to keep faith in you.
Though we cannot prove you rose again,
or that *we* will either,
may your voice continue to ring true within us,
speaking of your risen presence and promise of life:
a sure and certain hope.
Amen.

Silence

Comment

There's a sense in which we, as Christians, live in a state of limbo between the now and the not yet. We see God in part only, full knowledge of him being reserved for the future. We are part of this world but not of it, our hope lying in things beyond. We have received eternal life but face nonetheless the reality of death. The fulfilment of God's promises, the dawn of his kingdom, is yet to come. But that is not to say we are left in a state of suspended animation – far from it – for what *shall be* directly shapes what *is now*, our trust in God's promises directing the course and pattern of our life. During our time here on earth, there will always be much we do not understand, but through God's Spirit there will always also be enough revealed to us to give light to our path, illuminating the way ahead.

Music *(optional)*

Gloria (Coronation Mass) Mozart

Reading

John 13:31-36

Meditation of Thomas

We were confused when he first told us,
not to mention disappointed,
for we'd assumed somehow that he'd be with us always,
constantly there by our sides.
What was all this about leaving,
going where none of us could follow?
We didn't like such talk at all.
But if we were puzzled then,
it was as nothing to what came later,
after he rose again,
for just as we were celebrating his return,
beside ourselves with excitement,
he came up with the same refrain,
telling us he had to leave us once more.
'*Why*?' we wondered.
Couldn't he stay,
if not for ever then at least for a time?
What was so pressing,
so important,
that he had to disappear again,
and this time, apparently, for good?
We wanted to keep him with us,
to go back to how things had been before:
us and him together.
And so, as it turned out, we *have*,
though not quite in the way we thought,
for he's with us still through his Spirit,
not just by our side but within.
Only by leaving could he truly draw close.
Only through departing this earth
could he open the gates of heaven
that we might one day follow where he's gone
There could be no standing still or remaining the same,
for his place was with the Father
as King of kings and Lord of lords,
enthroned in glory on high.
We've learnt, finally, what that means:

that he's bigger than *us*,
bigger than Judea,
bigger than we'd ever imagined,
his dying and rising,
mercy and love,
being not just for a few
but for all.

Quiet reflection

Prayer

Forgive us, Lord,
for we tie you down to our own narrow horizons,
our limited parochial concerns.
We forget that you are exalted over all,
enthroned on high,
your purpose reaching to the ends of the earth
in every place and time.
Enlarge our vision,
broaden our understanding,
so that, in glimpsing your greatness,
we may recognise also the extent of your love –
the height, depth, length and breadth of who and what you are,
and what that means,
for us
and for all.
Amen.

Silent retreat

SECOND SESSION

Comment

We've spoken already of the way what we hope for helps to shape what we experience now, and that's equally the theme of our next reading and reflection. We listen first to words from John's Gospel – perhaps one of the best-loved passages in all Scripture – speaking of the joy God holds in store for us, and we move from there to consider the implications of Jesus' message for daily discipleship. Both are rich in promise.

Music *(optional)*

Spring Song in A Mendelssohn

Reading

John 14:23-29

Meditation of Philip

He'd talked of his Father's house,
of going there to prepare a place for us,
and that had seemed wonderful enough.
But then he went further,
and his words, if anything, were more wonderful,
more incredible still,
for he spoke of coming –
with the Father,
through his Spirit –
and making his home among us.
Imagine that:
God living *within*,
Jesus alive in our hearts,
divine love and power coursing through our veins!
It would change everything,
our thoughts, words and deeds,
making faith real in a way it's never been before.

Could it be possible,
sharing our life with the Lord of all,
walking and talking with the creator God –
mighty and majestic,
yet one with you and I?
It seemed too good to be true,
especially after they nailed him to a cross and sealed him in a tomb,
but it wasn't,
for he came back, just as he'd promised,
triumphant over the grave,
and now I know beyond doubt that he'll come again,
not just in the fullness of time
but in the here and now,
God indeed dwelling among us
if only we'll welcome him in.

Quiet reflection

Prayer

Lord Jesus Christ,
make your dwelling place within us.
Fill us with your Spirit
in heart, mind and soul
so that your living presence shapes who and what we are.
Come afresh into our lives,
and direct everything we think and say and do,
so that we shall live more fully as your people,
bringing glory to you.
Amen.

Silence

Comment

How do you picture heaven? Is it possible to picture it at all? Necessarily, we struggle to find words fit for the task since we're talking of something that transcends human experience and so defies definition. Yet, though any images we might come up with are hopelessly inadequate, though any descriptions are, at best, mere pointers to the truth, we nonetheless are not left entirely to guess, for our experiences of God's blessing now give us a clear idea of what he holds in store. Again, future and present combine, the one reinforcing the other.

Music *(optional)*

The trumpet shall sound (Messiah) Handel

Reading

John 17:20-26

Meditation of Andrew

We couldn't go where he was going,
he'd told us that before,
and though we didn't understand it at the time,
we did later,
for he was taken into heaven
to share in the Father's glory.
To be honest, we didn't *want* to go with him,
not if it meant leaving this world so soon for the next.
We'd a life to live
and a job to do:
the message of his love and purpose needing to be shared with others,
proclaimed throughout the world.
And after he rose again and was taken from us,
exalted by the Father,
we resolved to do just that:
to proclaim his love and work for his kingdom,
on earth as it is in heaven.
Yet, of course, this world,
for all its blessings,
is not an end in itself
but a taste of things to come,

and though we can't be with him now,
he's promised that one day we shall be,
each privileged to enter his kingdom
and witness his glory.
I can't say more –
no one can –
for though we've glimpsed a little,
our knowledge is incomplete,
but from what we've experienced already,
the love, joy and peace he's so richly given,
we know that his word is true,
his promise certain:
the best is yet to come.

Quiet reflection

Prayer

Thank you, Lord, for the wonder of life
and the beauty of this world –
so much around us that moves us to delight and wonder,
filling our hearts with praise.
Thank you for your presence with us in the here and now,
the way you so faithfully bless us
and give meaning to our lives.
But thank you, above all, for what you hold in store,
the joy that awaits us in your kingdom,
greater than anything our hearts can yet conceive,
special beyond words.
Amen.

Silent retreat

Closing comment

'Blessed be the God and Father of our Lord Jesus Christ! By his great mercy he has given us a new birth into a living hope through the resurrection of Jesus Christ from the dead.' Words of promise from 1 Peter 1:3 with which we began our thoughts today and that sum them up. We have been given hope that will not disappoint; the promise of a future extending beyond death for all eternity. Yet that does not mean turning our back on the present. On the contrary, it springs from our experience here and now of God's love and informs every moment of our lives, shaping the people we are – the way we think, speak and act. Though we will always struggle for words, and perhaps always also wrestle with questions, we can put our trust in God's promise, assured that nothing in heaven or earth, life or death, will ever be able to separate us from his everlasting love in Christ.

Closing prayer

Living God,
for the hope you have given us in Christ,
receive our praise,
our thanks
and our worship.
Teach us to live each day in the light of your promises,
celebrating every moment that you give us
and anticipating the blessings of your eternal kingdom –
those joys that no eye has seen
nor ear has heard,
nor human heart conceived,
prepared by your grace for all those who love you.
We put our trust in you,
now and always.
Amen.

Made whole

Suggested visual material

Jesus of Nazareth 3
The Life of Christ II

FIRST SESSION

Introduction

It's no exaggeration to say that the Church in recent years has rediscovered its healing role, not in any sensationalist sense, claiming to perform astonishing signs and wonders, but emphasising the wholeness of every individual, whatever their circumstances. We believe, of course, that in an ideal world God desires perfect health for everyone, but this world is far from ideal, all kind of factors frustrating his will and obstructing his purpose. Sometimes, despite this, he is able to bring astonishing physical healing, confounding doctors and sceptics alike. At other times, people have to learn to live with disability, illness, pain and even death itself, discovering wholeness even while they are broken.

This, however, is but one aspect of wholeness, the meaning of which extends much further. Some may be perfectly well physically yet troubled by fears and phobias that shatter their lives. Some wrestle with despair and depression, life seemingly devoid of joy. Others again find themselves spiritually empty, apparently having everything, yet yearning for some deeper reality that gives meaning to their lives. We all in some way hunger for wholeness, but are we ready to admit our need? Are we even aware what our needs are? Use this day to open your life to the searching presence of Christ and the touch of his hand. Use it to come quietly before him so that he may lead you towards the answers you seek, granting the wholeness of body, mind and spirit that he alone can bring.

Opening prayer

Lord Jesus Christ, reach out to us,
just as you did to so many during your earthly ministry.
Minister to us in our brokenness:
our inner yearning for meaning,
our sense of guilt and shame,
our struggle to love you and others,
our weakness of will,
our hurts and fears,
our pride, envy, greed and stubbornness –
so much that undermines life and devalues our humanity.
Minister to our broken world:
the sick and suffering,
the physically and mentally disabled,
the terminally ill;
victims of war,
the homeless and dispossessed;
the oppressed, exploited, vulnerable and poor;
so many crying out for help,
hope,
strength
and support.
Lord Jesus,
bring healing, we pray,
to us and to all,
and show us how we, in turn, can reach out in your name,
seeking to share your wholeness
and make known your love.
Amen.

Silence

Comment

We're going to reflect today on four incidents from the ministry of Jesus related to healing, each of which speaks in different ways of the wholeness he offers. Each raises as many questions as it answers. Each can be understood in various ways. The purpose of this day is not to tie up all the loose ends, providing a definition, explanation or analysis of the way God heals in Christ. Nor is it to try to unravel why some are not healed, despite their faith and prayers. Rather, it is to aid and encourage reflection; to give *us* the opportunity to listen to *God* and *God* the opportunity to speak to *us*.

First, then, the story of the Roman centurion's slave. What does it say about healing? And, more important, what does it say about Jesus?

Music *(optional)*

Libera me Domine (Requiem) Verdi

Reading

Luke 7:1-10

Meditation of the centurion's friends

1 He's a good man, our friend –
deserving, if anyone is, of total respect.
2 And believe me, that's some compliment,
for we don't usually have time for *Romans*, us Jews!
3 But, you see, this man was different,
a cut apart from the rest.
1 Take the way he treated his slave:
3 he really *cared* for him –
enough, when the poor man fell ill, to send word to Jesus,
begging him to come and help.
2 Such compassion is rare, I can tell you.
1 Yet the strange thing is,
no sooner had he made the request,
than he seemed overwhelmed,
3 almost embarrassed,
2 as though the prospect of meeting Jesus was too much,
the honour too great!

1 So he despatched us to send Jesus back,
confident, apparently, that he could heal from afar.
2 Who was this man to inspire such faith;
to cause someone so plainly commendable
to feel unworthy even to share the same roof?
3 We wondered,
1 we puzzled,
2 troubled and confused,
3 expecting on our return to find the slave dead.
1 But we didn't,
for our master had been right:
the man *was* healed,
2 fully restored,
3 one word from Jesus enough to make him well.
1 We were astounded,
2 gobsmacked –
3 staggered beyond words!
2 But our friend wasn't –
not surprised in the slightest.
1 A good man, like I say,
worthy of praise,
3 but in Jesus, that day, we found someone more deserving,
more special still:
2 a man who brought healing and wholeness –
deliverance from death.
1 You don't get many who'd do that, I was about to say,
but, of course, that's wrong.
All Apart from him, so far as we know,
you don't get *any*!

Quiet reflection

Prayer

Lord Jesus Christ,
save us from ever forgetting how special you are –
from thinking of you merely as a good man,
a great teacher,

but essentially like *us* nonetheless.
Remind us that you brought healing,
forgiveness,
new beginnings,
turning people's lives around,
and that you go on doing so day after day.
Not just a good man,
but an extraordinary one,
God made flesh –
nothing like us at all!
Amen.

Silence

Comment

The character in our next story would, I suspect, be diagnosed by psychiatrists today as schizophrenic. Mentally and spiritually he was clearly deeply disturbed in ways that few of us, thankfully, will ever experience. But don't be fooled into thinking that this incident, in consequence, has nothing to say to you, for you couldn't be more wrong. The ministry Jesus offered here was simple but vital; quite simply, one of loving acceptance. That is a gift we all need to receive and to share.

Music *(optional)*

Calm me, Lord (Fire of Love) Margaret Rizza

Reading

Luke 8:26-39

Meditation of the Gerasene man healed by Jesus

I didn't know who I was,
literally,
for a multitude of voices competed in my head,
each screaming for attention.

It drove me mad –
the confusion,
the pulling this way and that,
not knowing from one moment to the next which face I would wear,
which person I would be.
No wonder people were scared of me,
for in my more lucid moments I was afraid of *myself* –
of what I might do or become.
But then I met Jesus –
and everything changed.
He saw who I *really* was:
not the monster running wild in the hills,
the tortured misfit torn between competing identities,
but a unique individual,
a human being with as much worth and potential as any other.
He reached out to me in a way no one had done before,
offering love and acceptance,
seeing the person behind the façade,
and in so doing he helped me face up to myself –
to confront my inner demons and start again.
Have *you* done that:
found real and lasting peace?
Have you learnt to value yourself as much as God does?
You may not be as mixed up as I was,
as troubled in mind and spirit,
but you're probably not *untroubled* either,
as free as you'd like to be from the demons that haunt you –
the voices of fear, doubt, guilt and despair that,
night and day,
whisper within.
Don't run from them,
for they'll always give chase.
Don't wrestle on your own,
for their hold is strong.
Turn to Jesus
and find rest for your soul.

Quiet reflection

Prayer

To all whose minds are troubled, Lord,
who wrestle with fear,
worry,
depression
or mental illness,
bring help and healing.
Speak your word of peace,
and may they find in you acceptance and understanding,
quietness of mind
and rest for their soul.
Amen.

Silent retreat

SECOND SESSION

Comment

We're aware today, as perhaps never before, of the importance of holistic therapies; in other words, treating the whole person rather than just the outward symptoms of an illness. Body, mind and spirit are interdependent, and when one suffers all can suffer. We glimpse just that in some of the Gospel accounts of healing, it being difficult to identify at times just where the root of a person's problem actually lies. On one thing Jesus is clear: ill health is not sent by God as punishment for wrongdoing. But it's equally clear that spiritual or emotional malaise can have physical implications. So it seems to be for the woman in the following story, but was she the only one in need of healing, the only one whose growth had been stunted? Once again here we're reminded that wholeness has a wider meaning than we may imagine.

Music *(optional)*

Life of Christ renew me (River of Peace) Margaret Rizza

Reading

Luke 13:10-17

Meditation of the woman healed by Jesus

He helped me to walk tall,
literally!
For the first time in years I could hold my head up in public,
meet people eye to eye –
and it was truly wonderful.
But it wasn't just my body he set free,
it was my mind and spirit,
for there too,
more than I ever realised,
I'd been imprisoned,
crippled by a false view of life:
of myself, the world and God.
Mind you, I wasn't the only one,
not by a long way.
Take that leader of the synagogue:
though he couldn't see it,
he was in a worse state still.
Believe it or not, he was furious when Jesus healed me,
absolutely livid.
And why?
Because it was the sabbath,
the day of rest.
Ridiculous, isn't it,
but he was genuinely incensed,
convinced Jesus had committed some mortal sin,
an affront against God,
by putting my welfare first.
The terrible thing is he was sincere,
his indignation all too real.

Tragic!
Don't let that happen to you.
However strong your convictions,
don't put them before people.
However firm your beliefs,
don't put them before God.
It's the spirit of the Law that matters, not the letter –
lose sight of that and you've lost everything.
Argue if you like,
but one thing I know:
Jesus saw my need
and set me free.
How about you?

Quiet reflection

Prayer

Redeemer Christ,
save us from turning faith into rules and regulations,
a matter of outward observance,
doing things by the book.
Guard us from intolerant and inflexible attitudes,
from being preoccupied with incidentals
rather than with what really counts –
a life lived for you.
Help us to celebrate the freedom you died to bring,
rather than to impose,
on ourselves and others,
fresh burdens of our own.
Amen.

Silence

Comment

A common feature of the incidents we've looked at is that they point beyond the actual healing recorded to wider questions of wholeness, and so it is again with our final example. On the surface it's simply an account of ten lepers being made well, but look deeper and two more fundamental issues emerge. One is that of a society which, for all kinds of reasons, dismisses the worth of others; a broken world, with its commensurate attitudes, in need of healing. The other is recognising our need of God and acknowledging where wholeness truly lies; whether we take his gift for granted or acknowledge what we owe.

Music *(optional)*

Ode to joy Beethoven

Reading

Luke 17:11-19

Meditation of Matthew

They were healed, all ten of them –
their skin made clean,
their lives transformed –
and you'd have thought, wouldn't you,
that they'd have rushed back immediately,
desperate to thank the man who'd made them well?
But they didn't,
most instead dashing off as fast as their legs would carry them,
without even a backward glance.
They were excited, I suppose,
impatient to return to their loved ones and share the news,
and, heaven knows, I can understand that,
for they'd been through misery such as you can scarcely imagine.
It seemed rude, nonetheless,
for they owed Jesus so much
yet couldn't be bothered to acknowledge the debt.

All, that is, except one.
He stopped, incredulous,
the moment he realised what had happened . . .
then turned and hurried back,
glorifying and praising God,
throwing himself at the Master's feet with tears of joy,
thankful beyond words.
And do you know what?
He was a *Samaritan*!
That's right,
the last person you'd expect according to popular opinion:
an outsider,
foreigner,
heretic.
It reinforced what we knew already:
that Jesus has time for those the world doesn't.
But it brought home also the flipside of the coin:
that those we least expect have time for *him*,
gladly responding where others don't.
I shouldn't have needed reminding, of course,
for it's true among his closest followers –
me included! –
yet how often do we write people off,
failing to see who they really are?
Don't make that mistake,
putting restrictions on God's love and purpose.
Don't let prejudice close your mind.
Learn to look, as Jesus does,
beyond the label to the person underneath.
What you find may surprise you.

Quiet reflection

Prayer

When we're tempted to dismiss people, Lord,
unable to see past their faults;
when prejudice and preconceptions dictate our attitudes,

closing our minds to those around us,
remind us that you refuse to give up on anyone,
determined instead to seek until you find.
Open our hearts to the potential of others,
the worth you see in all,
lest in rejecting *them*
we reject *you*.
Amen.

Silent retreat

Closing comment

We are all less than whole – that is part of being human – and faith offers no guarantee of miraculous healing. What it *does* promise is that God cares about us – body, mind and spirit – and is able, like none other, to minister to the whole person bringing strength, comfort, hope, help and renewal. Are we open to our need? Are we open to Christ's touch? And what does that mean for you?

Closing prayer

Where lives are broken, Lord,
mend them.
Where there is sickness and disease,
bring healing.
Where minds are disturbed,
give peace.
Where there is pain and suffering,
grant relief.
Where there is yearning for meaning,
offer guidance.
Through your healing touch,
grant true wholeness deep within.
Amen.

Costly commitment

Suggested visual material

Jesus of Nazareth 5–6
The Life of Christ III
Oberammergau 1990
Man of the Cross
He Carries our Cross

FIRST SESSION

Introduction

If anyone would come after me, said Jesus (Luke 9:23), let them deny themselves, take up their cross and follow me – words that leave anybody contemplating Christian discipleship in no doubt that commitment involves cost. But how seriously do we take that warning? How far, if at all, does our allegiance to Christ actually cost us *anything*? It's not, of course, that we should look to make martyrs of ourselves – any such attempt would run contrary to the whole spirit of the gospel – but if our commitment is authentic then, necessarily, it will at times involve difficult demands and decisions.

Today, through focusing on four passages from the Gospel of Luke, we're going to reflect on what some of those demands and decisions might be. They may speak directly to your situation. They may suggest entirely different possibilities – other aspects of discipleship where you're conscious of evading the challenge of Jesus or diluting the force of his call. Let God guide your thoughts as he will, through words, through silence; and through these too let us make our response, consecrating ourselves afresh to serving Christ and walking his way.

Opening prayer

Loving God,
we have come today seeking your guidance,
for though we long to serve you
our commitment is weak
and our faith is poor.
Meet with us now, in this time we have set aside,
and speak through the words we will hear
and silence we will share.
Teach us more of what it means to follow Christ,
to honour him in thought, word and deed.
Challenge us where we are lacking.
Correct us where we have gone astray.
Instruct us where we have misunderstood.
Forgive us where we resist your will.
Move among us through your Spirit,
and grant the encouragement and inspiration we need
to walk more faithfully the way of your Son,
by his grace
and in his strength.
Amen.

Comment

We begin with one of the most celebrated followers of Jesus: the Apostle Peter. He, you'll recall, challenged Jesus concerning the need for him to suffer and die, only to be rebuked with the words 'Get behind me, Satan!' (Matthew 16:23). And in the years to follow he was to learn through often painful experience, culminating in his own crucifixion, of the cost that discipleship can involve. Did he understand those implications when Jesus first called him? Almost certainly not. Would it have made any difference had he done so? Who can say? But despite the cost, if you could have spoken to him at the end of his life, would he have had any regrets about responding to Christ's call. Ask yourself that, as you listen to this reading and subsequent reflection upon it.

Music *(optional)*

Traveller's prayer (Sacred Pathway) Keith Duke

Reading

Luke 5:1-11

Meditation of Simon Peter

He called me to follow,
to lay down my nets and follow him.
No time to think,
to weigh up the pros and cons;
then and there, the need to decide.
So I did,
on the spot –
left everything to become one of his disciples.
And I'm glad.
No, honestly, despite everything, I'm glad,
for it's been worth it, a hundred times over.
Yet had I understood at very beginning what would be asked of me,
it might have been a different story,
very different indeed,
because, looking back,
I realise I had little idea just what I was taking on.
I imagined he wanted me to accompany him for a few days,
weeks at most,
and then, having done my bit, I could return home,
back to friends and family,
back to the security of my fishing nets,
back to the way things had always been –
but he soon put me right on that, didn't he?
He made it quite clear that discipleship is a lifelong commitment,
not an option you can walk away from as the mood takes you.
Well, a few of us soon considered chucking it in,
cutting our losses before we got in too deep.
Only we couldn't do that,
not when it came to it,

for we knew that, though he was asking much,
he was offering more.
He had the answers we were looking for,
the words of eternal life,
and to have walked away then
would have been to turn our backs
on our one true chance of happiness.
So we carried on,
day after day,
week after week,
month after month,
following in his footsteps,
sharing in his work.
And it was tough going, I can tell you,
really tough –
believe me, as a fisherman I know what I'm talking about.
Yet somehow we always found the strength we needed,
just as he said we would,
or at least we did until that awful last week
when suddenly it all went wrong –
the week Judas betrayed him,
the soldiers arrested him,
Pilate condemned him;
the week when we all ran for our lives,
our love and loyalty forgotten.
It was terrible,
more dreadful than my worst nightmares –
I've never known fear or sorrow like I felt then,
and I asked myself as never before,
'Why did I ever get mixed up with Jesus?'
I still ask that sometimes, more often than you might imagine,
for it's not got any easier following him.
There've been sacrifices to make,
suffering to endure,
rejection to face,
and I know that one day, unless I'm much mistaken,
I shall pay the ultimate price.
So yes, if I'd known then what I know now

I might have decided differently.
It's possible – I really don't know –
but I'm glad I didn't,
for though it's been difficult and invariably demanding,
it's been wonderful also,
and I know not only was it the right decision,
it was the best I could ever have made.

Quiet reflection

Prayer

Lord Jesus Christ,
help us to follow you like your disciples of old –
to respond to your call
and walk where you lead.
In the journey of faith,
whatever its ups and down,
costs or rewards,
may our commitment stay strong,
our trust real
and our service vibrant,
your strength sufficient for all our needs.
May we run our race to the end,
not just for the joy set before us
but for that of knowing you now,
always and everywhere by our side.
Amen.

Silence

Comment

Few of us like to be thought of as different, least of all in a negative sense, so when following Jesus involves taking a stand, we find it hard. Recognised or otherwise, we face a constant pressure to conform, to go along with the way of the world, accepting its assumptions and values. To challenge those takes courage, risking unpopularity, scorn or even hostility. Far easier to compromise, tone things down, and that's just what many of us can unconsciously end up doing. It may be the most comfortable option, but it's not the way of Christ.

Music *(optional)*

Lord of my life (Fountain of Life) Margaret Rizza

Reading

Luke 6:17-26

Meditation of the Apostle John

We were puzzled, I don't mind telling you,
for why should we be concerned instead of pleased
when people think well of us?
Surely if we live up to what Jesus asks of us,
loving our enemies,
responding to those in need,
we're bound to create a good impression.
Well perhaps,
perhaps not,
for, as we came to learn,
truly following Jesus involves rather more.
It means rejecting the way of the world,
refusing to conform.
It means speaking the truth in love,
even though truth may hurt.
It means speaking out against evil,
and standing up for what we believe.
All this,
and much more,
can be harder than we might think,
costing us money,
comfort,

opportunities,
friends.
Far easier to go along with the crowd,
compromise our convictions,
water down our faith;
to tell people what they want to hear,
seeking approval at the cost of truth.
It's true that faith will win its admirers,
but it will win its cynics too,
its mockers,
its enemies,
just as Jesus found,
and much though you might wish it were otherwise,
if you've never encountered any of those
then it might be time to ask whether the faith you profess
is really faith at all.

Quiet reflection

Prayer

Living Lord,
though faith in you arouses scorn,
though serving you involves sacrifice,
though commitment to you meets with hostility
and though honouring you proves demanding,
help us to stay true to you,
faithful to our calling whatever life may bring.
Amen.

Silent retreat

SECOND SESSION

Comment

One piece of advice we'll all have been given is 'Read the small print', and we'll all know from painful experience how important it is to do just that. We take out an insurance policy, only to find we're not covered when it comes to making a claim, some tiny clause we couldn't be bothered to look at rendering our case an exception. We invest some money or take out a mortgage, believing we've covered all the angles, only to be caught out when the market plunges and we discover markets can go down as well as up. We click on a licence agreement online, assuming it's a routine sign-up procedure, only to discover that we're committed to a costly contract from which there's no escape. There may not be an overt attempt to defraud us, but, at the very least, less desirable truths are pushed carefully out of view in the hope that we'll overlook them. No such accusation could be levelled against Jesus. Time and again during the course of his ministry he made clear to the disciples the challenge of what they were taking on, the potential costliness of discipleship, and nowhere more so is that true than when he sent the apostles out to speak and work in his name.

Music *(optional)*

Pilgrims' Chorus (Tannhäuser) Wagner

Reading

Luke 10:1-11, 16-20

Meditation of Luke

Sheep among wolves –
not much of a prospect, is it?
But give Jesus this,
he tells things straight,
honest to a fault.

He could have dressed things up,
pretended commitment is easy,
but he didn't,
leaving us instead under no illusions
about what discipleship may cost.
Not that it's all doom and gloom.
We'll be encouraged sometimes,
our message welcomed,
but such moments will be the exception rather than the rule,
anomalies that buck the trend.
We don't like that idea, do we?
For we want respect,
popularity,
success,
acclaim.
But such goals reflect *our* way of thinking
rather than *God's*.
If we're faithful to the gospel in word and deed,
witnessing through the people we are to the challenge of Christ,
then for every positive response we receive
there will be far more that are negative,
for every Yes, a string of Nos.
Don't lose heart, then, when the road is tough,
when commitment asks much yet seems to deliver little.
It's not an easy way to live,
but it's the *only* way to *life*.

Quiet reflection

Prayer

Lord Jesus Christ,
give us courage to walk your way,
even when it is demanding,
costly.
Help us stand up for our faith
and speak out for you,
resisting the temptation to go along with the world.

Remind us that though we may forfeit prosperity or popularity,
we will gain far more,
a life at one with you.
Amen.

Silence

Comment

The words of Jesus can be positively disturbing at times, and need to be interpreted with care. Those of our next reading are a case in point, for they could all too easily be used to justify one of the worst aspects of sectarian religion: splits and feuds among family and friends. Some fringe religious groups encourage such division, seeing it as a test of faith and demonstration of loyalty, and there's no denying that on occasions during his ministry Jesus seemed to show ambivalence towards his family. Yet if that's so, it was only to avoid the risk of people misunderstanding who he was and what he came to do. There may be times when our convictions lead to conflict within the home, but those are the exception rather than the rule, to be contemplated only as a last resort. Jesus is not advocating division here, but emphasising the importance of putting God first in our lives; even, if necessary, before our nearest and dearest if loyalty to them stands in the way of following him.

Music *(optional)*

Jesus is our joy (Fire of Love) Margaret Rizza

Reading

Luke 14:25-33

Meditation of Mary, mother of Jesus

Hate father and mother!
What can he mean?
For he doesn't hate *me*, that's for sure.

He may seem curt, sometimes,
even cold,
for he's preoccupied by the burden of ministry –
the demands,
the pressure,
the cost –
but he cares about my welfare as much as any son cares for his mum,
and more besides.
So what's this talk of his, so stark and shocking?
I don't understand.
But wait . . .
perhaps I do . . .
for both Joseph and I saw early on that nothing –
nothing at all –
would deflect him from his calling;
that if it were a choice between serving us or God,
then God would always win.
He wouldn't oppose us if he could help it,
still less cause unhappiness,
but if we or anyone else stood in the way of right,
of what he believed must be done,
then he would make a stand, come what may.
That's what he means, surely:
not that we should *hate* anyone
but that we must love God more than all,
putting him even before those we hold most dear
if serving *them* means betraying *him*.
It's a question of what matters most,
where our ultimate allegiance lies,
and whether, if – God forbid – you're put to the test,
you'll take the easy way,
or the hard.

Quiet reflection

Prayer

Teach us, Lord, to love others,
but none too much;
to seek the good of those we hold dear,
but never to put them before you.
Help us to be true in all our relationships,
but to recognise when we must choose between them,
lest we end up betraying all.
Amen.

Silent retreat

Closing comment

Our readings today and reflections upon them boil down to a simple question: who comes first in our lives? What matters most: the opinion of others, or how God sees us? Serving self or serving him? The question is not a stark either/or, a harsh dichotomy between one or the other, but moments will nonetheless come when, faced with tough choices, we have to make up our minds; when *true* commitment means costly commitment. For Jesus, honouring God's call meant giving everything. What are we ready to give in return?

Closing prayer

Lord Jesus Christ,
we have committed ourselves to you
and yearn to follow faithfully,
but your way can be hard,
more demanding that we imagined.
It challenges our complacency,
asking questions of us we'd rather not face,
calling us to stand up and be counted,
to choose between you and the world;
to give and go on giving,
love and go on loving,

putting you first,
others next,
and self last.
Forgive our struggle to do that,
our avoiding or watering down of your message
when discipleship proves costly.
Help us to remember that whatever you ask of us,
you offer far more,
life in all its fullness.
Send us out, then, in your name,
strengthened in faith,
refreshed in spirit
and renewed in commitment,
ready to live and work in your name
and to your glory.
Amen.

Whose way?

Suggested visual material

Jesus of Nazareth 4
The Life of Christ II

FIRST SESSION

Opening prayer

Living God,
we have come seeking your word,
your way,
your will.
As we listen together to the Scriptures
and reflect upon them,
as we join together in prayer,
and as we make time and space for quiet contemplation,
speak,
challenge,
inspire
and guide.
Show us what it means to know and serve you,
to walk the way of Christ,
and equip us, through being here today,
to do so more faithfully,
to the glory of your name.
Amen.

Introduction

We talk rather glibly sometimes of the way of Christ, as though it's unmistakably different from that of the world. It should be, of course, but in practice what is there to distinguish Christian discipleship from the way others live their lives? In what ways could and should we be distinctive? Today we're going to explore four possible answers to that question, words of Jesus pointing to the qualities we're called to show, the attributes that should set us apart and characterise our commitment. And we turn first to one of the most challenging passages anywhere: words from the Sermon on the Mount that stand the world's values and expectations on their head. If we could live up to this challenge alone, what an impact our witness would make.

Music *(optional)*

Come, my way (River of Peace) Margaret Rizza

Reading

Luke 6:20-31

Meditation of a Christian in the early Church

Love your enemies?
Turn the other cheek?
Give without counting the cost?
How many can do that, I ask you?
I couldn't.
Yet plenty I've seen have done as much and more,
renouncing this world and its comforts,
reaching out to those who persecute them,
day after day meeting hatred with love and evil with good.
Stephen,
Peter,
Andrew,
James –
they've gone the same way,
and countless others like them,
giving their service,
their lives,
their all
for the sake of Christ.

All right, so perhaps their stories have been embellished,
none of them quite the unblemished saints we paint them,
yet, for all that, their lives put mine to shame,
displaying faith I can only dream of,
commitment that exposes my feeble counterpart as empty posturing,
a playing at discipleship.
How did they do it?
Through iron will,
or some innate goodness inherited from birth?
Neither of those.
It was one thing, pure and simple:
knowing and loving Jesus deep in their hearts.
That's the secret of their strength:
not some steely resolve or genetic trait,
but the one whose example they follow,
who gave himself for them,
showing what loving, giving and caring is all about.
We revere them as martyrs,
saints of God,
but they'd shake their heads, puzzled at the idea,
for to them they're only giving back to him who offered more.
They sacrificed much,
and if I fail to understand why,
or to know the one they did it for,
then it's not *them* that's the loser . . .
it's *me*.

Quiet reflection

Prayer

Speak, Lord, through those who have run the race before us,
all who have kept the faith to their journey's end.
Speak, especially, through those
who have shown courage and commitment beyond the norm.
Encourage and inspire us through their love for you,
their willingness to take up their cross,

and so help us, in turn, to follow you more faithfully,
love you more deeply
and honour you more completely.
Amen.

Silence

Comment

Our next reading and subsequent meditation revolves around a saying so familiar that we can forget it originated with Jesus. We'd all wholeheartedly endorse its sentiments, or at least so we like to think, but is that actually true? It pays to reflect on what's being said here and to ask whether we've fully understood what Jesus was getting at. Apply his words to our lives, act upon them, and we will indeed be seen to be different.

Music *(optional)*

In nominee (Sacred Weave) Keith Duke

Reading

Luke 6:27-38

Meditation of a listener to Jesus

Do as you would be done by.
Now that's an idea I can get my head round,
one that I'm more than happy to follow.
None of that 'love your enemies' stuff,
'turn the other cheek',
'give to those who beg' –
just sound common-sense advice.
It's what most of us do anyway, isn't it?
Treat people fair and they'll be fair with you.

Only, he seems to mean there's more to it than that,
for he's back on his bandwagon:
forgive,
judge not,
do good to all,
as though those are part of the same thought,
each belonging together.
He's right of course,
for that's how I'd want others to treat me.
I'd expect them to make allowances when I make mistakes,
to forgive and forget if I'm truly sorry.
I'd look for understanding of my actions,
a fair hearing rather than jumping to conclusions,
condemning out of hand.
And, should I be in need, I'd hope for kindness,
help,
support.
Yet how many times, if I'm honest,
have I nursed a grievance,
leapt to pass judgement
and ignored the needy –
thoughts only for myself?
I do it all the time,
loving where I'm loved,
giving as I receive,
my reaction towards others depending on theirs towards me
'Do to others as you would have them do to you' –
it sounds so straightforward,
so sensible,
but, taken seriously, it's harder than it sounds.
So often we do, not as we *would* be done by,
but as we *have* been –
and there's a world of difference between the two.

Quiet reflection

Prayer

Forgive, Lord, our knee-jerk reactions to others,
our instinctive desire to extract an eye for an eye
and a tooth for a tooth.
Forgive us for failing to see in ourselves
the wrongs we see in them;
for expecting allowances to be made for *our* faults
yet refusing to make them in turn.
Help us truly to do to others what we'd have done to us,
giving though we do not receive,
loving though no love is returned,
remembering that for us who deserve so little
you gave so much.
Amen.

Silent retreat

SECOND SESSION

Comment

One aspect of life Jesus frequently commented on – and one aspect of his teaching we often prefer to ignore – concerns our stewardship of money and possessions. Set your heart, he tells us, on treasure in heaven, not riches on earth, and we nod sagely in agreement, but how many of us can honestly claim to put those words into practice? Of course, money and possessions are not intrinsically wrong in themselves, but both can all too easily end up owning us instead of us them. In this session, then, we're going to listen to and reflect on two passages from the Gospel of Luke, both of which speak of the way we understand and use our financial resources. What do they say to you, and what is your response to God?

Music *(optional)*

Jesu, joy of man's desiring J. S. Bach

Reading

Luke 12:32-40

Meditation of one of the crowd listening to Jesus

A purse that never wears out –
now I like the sound of that!
Just imagine:
pop your hand in your pocket,
any time,
anywhere,
and there it is,
cash on the nail,
as much as you need.
This guy's really talking!
Only he isn't,
for his sums don't add up.
'Sell your possessions,' he says,
'and give alms.'
Well, I'm sorry, but that's no way to invest for the future.
You'll end up, more like, with nothing,
relying on alms yourself,
and we can't *all* do that, can we,
for who'd be left then to give?
So what's he saying?
Don't tell me:
it's about letting go, isn't it?
About hanging loose to money and possessions;
about understanding what's of real value,
able to satisfy the soul;
and, most of all, about receiving through giving,
a generous heart compared to an avaricious spirit.
I was afraid you'd say that,
for though I can accept it happily enough in theory,
in practice it's another matter,
neither *my* way nor that of the world.
We want treasure now *and* later,
rewards in this life *and* the life to come,

our hearts torn between God and self,
heaven and earth,
both/and rather than *either/or*.
I'll give Jesus this,
he's put his finger on the problem,
but that's the easy part.
It needs us to change, deep within,
if we're to find the answer;
our hearts to be realigned,
turned around.
Can he see to that too?

Quiet reflection

Prayer

Loving Lord,
we mean to be generous,
but find it hard to let go;
we mean to respond to others,
but struggle to put *them* first, *self* second.
For all our talk of treasure in heaven
it's treasures on earth that consume us . . .
even as we consume them!
Work within us,
and overcome our greed.
Help us to see beyond the flesh to the spirit,
in a world where so many,
all too literally,
can barely keep body and soul together.
Amen.

Music *(optional)*

Take, Lord (Awakening in Love) Margaret Rizza

Reading

Luke 16:1-13

Meditation of a modern-day Christian

What does he mean, 'dishonest wealth'?
He's barking up the wrong tree there,
for my money has been fairly earned,
legal and above board.
Only it's not that simple, is it,
for who can say what deals it's financed,
palms greased,
services bought,
or wrongs contributed to?
It may seem innocent enough, the cash in my pocket,
yet it's a dangerous thing,
to be handled with caution,
not necessarily the root of all evil in itself,
but soon becoming so should we love it too much.
And as I thought about those words of Jesus –
really thought –
I realised I do just that,
for I found myself increasingly uncomfortable,
trying to water down,
explain away,
what I'd rather not hear.
I talk of using my money wisely,
giving to those in need,
but more often than not my charity starts at home . . .
and stays there.
I talk of fair trade,
ethical investment,
yet far too frequently it's *all* talk and nothing more.
Time and again, as Jesus warned, I attempt to serve two masters,
and no prizes for guessing, when the two clash, which one wins.
I may *get* my money fairly,
but do I *use* it fairly as well?

That's the question.
The first is easy enough.
The second not easy at all.

Quiet reflection

Prayer

Forgive us, Lord,
for we are part of an unjust and unequal world,
a world in which *we* have plenty at the cost of others.
Help us to do what we can to redress the balance,
not just through giving to charity,
but through using our money wisely
so that it contributes towards change.
Though economic issues are complex
save us from hiding behind them;
from foolishly believing we can both have our cake and eat it,
serving *self* as well as you.
Amen.

Silent retreat

Closing comment

Whose way do we follow? That of Christ or the world? We may have no doubt about the answer, but that's not what finally counts. The question is, does our allegiance show? Do others see anything about our lives that is distinctive, testifying to the faith we proclaim? That doesn't mean being different for the sake of it, still less being odd or eccentric. What it does mean is that Christian commitment should in some way show. Does ours?

Closing prayer

Go with us, Lord,
in our hearts,
our minds,
our souls,
so that what we think and do and say points to you –
so that who and what we are speaks of your joy,
your peace,
your grace
and your goodness –
a testimony to your love.
Show us your way,
and help us to walk it.
Amen.

Searching questions

Suggested visual material

Jesus of Nazareth 4
The Life of Christ II

FIRST SESSION

Introduction

Do you have queries about your faith? If you haven't, something is probably wrong, for questions are integral to the way we learn, and hence grow, as people. We ask them when we're young, wanting to know now this, now that, hungry to understand how the world works, why things happen, not to mention the whats, wheres and whens of life. And as we get older we *answer* questions; for example, in exams, or responding to our own children's thirst for knowledge. Usually the answers are straightforward enough. At times though, when we're pondering the deeper questions of life, they can be hugely complicated, definitive solutions consistently eluding us. But even then, the very act of questioning is important in itself: part of our continuing search for understanding.

In this session, we're going to reflect on some of the questions *God* asks of *us* – searching questions about the way we live and what we live for. Then, in the second session, we're going to move on to some of the questions we might ask of God; aspects of life and faith we wrestle with even while holding them dear. Use each of the readings and meditations as a means towards allowing God to search you, and you to search for him, opening the way for your faith to grow stronger and deeper by being stretched.

Opening prayer

Loving God,
we want to know you better:
to understand more of your will,
grasp more fully the nature of your love,
comprehend the length, breadth, height and depth
of who and what you are.
We want to learn of your way,
your kingdom,
your grace,
your truth;
to grow in faith so that we may walk more closely with you.
Search us,
and challenge our flawed assumptions or mistaken beliefs.
Teach us,
and grant us true wisdom.
Answer us,
and when we truly seek,
help us to find.
Take this day,
and draw us closer to you through all that we shall share.
Amen.

Comment

First, then, a question put to Jesus that ended up being turned back on the questioner, forcing a wholesale rethink concerning faith and life. The story is familiar enough – perhaps too familiar. Don't let that stop you hearing God's question to you.

Music *(optional)*

Fire of love (Fire of Love) Margaret Rizza

Reading

Luke 10:25-37

Meditation of the lawyer who questioned Jesus

'Teacher,' I said, 'what must I do to inherit eternal life?'
and I knew what he was going to say, even as I put the question.
It was typical of the man's genius,
always turning the tables on those who tried to catch him out.
'What is written in the law?' he asked. 'What do you read there?'
Brilliant!
Only this time, I believed, he would meet his match,
for I was well used to legal debate,
and had my case prepared.
'Love God,' I said, 'love your neighbour.'
'Exactly,' he said, 'do this and you will live,'
as though that was that,
the discussion at an end,
But that was my cue,
and I leapt in gleefully,
sensing the kill.
'Yes,' I smirked, 'but who is my neighbour?'
Clever, don't you think?
And I genuinely believed I had him stumped,
for though all this loving of neighbour sounds fair enough,
what does it actually mean?
If you've never asked yourself that then it's time you did,
for how wide should we spread the net –
when or where should we draw the line?
The people next door, they're our neighbours obviously,
but what about those in our village, our town, our country,
let alone those beyond?
Where does it start?
Where does it end?
You tell me.
And that's the question I put to Jesus,
fully expecting him to flounder in my well-laid trap.
Come on, I reasoned, there have to be limits somewhere!
The Romans, for example,
our hated oppressors –
surely he couldn't mean them!

And as for tax-collectors, prostitutes, sinners,
you could write them off for certain –
accept them and we'd be talking of Samaritans next,
our enemies –
God forbid!
No, I had him pinned down,
his back to the wall,
and there could surely be no escape?
Only then he looked at me,
and told that unforgettable story about, you've guessed it . . .
a *Samaritan*! –
and somehow the question was back where it had started:
with *me*.
'Which of these three was a neighbour to the man?' he asked,
his meaning all too clear,
and it was clear then, beyond any doubt,
that he meant what he said;
that he seriously wants us to treat *everyone* as our neighbour –
no person outside our concern,
no situation we can wash our hands of.
I'd put the question,
I'd had my answer,
and, I tell you what,
I wish I'd never asked!

Quiet reflection

Prayer

Open our hearts, Lord, to our neighbours everywhere
and our responsibilities towards them.
In the hunger of the poor,
the misery of the homeless,
and the plight of the refugee;
in the despair of the oppressed
and anger of the exploited;
in the victims of natural disaster, terrorism, violence and war;

help us to recognise your call,
your need,
our summons to loving response.
Amen.

Silence

Comment

Our next reading doesn't seem at first sight to be a question at all, but it *is* nonetheless, and a very deep question at that. Behind the parable of the rich man and his barns is a challenge to us all concerning our priorities, our values, our *raison d'être*. In just a few words Jesus asks us all: on what is our life based and where does our hope really lie?

Music *(optional)*

You are the centre (Chants and Songs) Margaret Rizza

Reading

Luke 12:13-21

Meditation of a listener to Jesus

He didn't mean me, I decided.
Well, he couldn't do, could he?
For I wasn't rich,
not by a mile,
and though I wouldn't have minded a bit extra in my pocket,
the occasional luxury at home,
I could hardly be termed greedy either.
No, he must have had others in mind,
people who are always after more –
you know the sort I mean.

Only I thought afterwards about what he'd said,
about there being more than one type of greed,
and suddenly I wasn't so sure he didn't mean me after all,
for I'm greedy in all kinds of ways –
for happiness,
security,
success,
comfort,
to name but some –
and though there's nothing wrong with those in themselves,
there is if we try to turn them into possessions,
as though we can cling hold of them,
make them our own.
We just can't do that,
not in this life,
and if we look for meaning in this world alone
it will surely slip from our grasp,
like sand running through our fingers.
On what is our life based?
That's the question he was asking.
The things of God,
or of earth?
We can possess much yet have nothing,
own little but have all.
True contentment is in God's hands;
whether we find it in *ours*.

Quiet reflection

Prayer

Forgive us, Lord,
for we spend so much of our lives chasing illusory happiness,
thirsting for what can never satisfy,
pursuing riches on earth rather than treasure in heaven.
Help us to grasp where true fulfilment lies,
and to recognise that if we work for the things of your kingdom

with even a fraction of the effort we put into gaining worldly wealth,
we will find contentment indeed.
Amen.

Silent retreat

SECOND SESSION

Comment

If there's one area of faith you have questions about, it probably concerns resurrection and eternal life. It's central to our commitment and at the heart of the gospel – the truth that alone makes sense of everything – but though we joyfully accept it, we struggle to get our heads round the how, what, why, where and when. So much here is necessarily a mystery, leaving us tongue-tied when questioned by others and bemused when looking for answers. As the following reading and meditations remind us, we're not the only ones to have questions. How, though, do we deal with them?

Music *(optional)*

Credo (Mass in B minor) J. S. Bach

Reading

Luke 20:27-38

Meditation of the Apostle John

They tried to tie him in knots with their questions,
coming to him with some fanciful conundrum
about marriage in the world to come,
It was a fair enough point on the surface,
but it depended on one assumption:
that life in heaven will mirror our existence here on earth.

Is that how you see it?
It's hard not to, isn't it,
for what other experience do we have to go on?
However high our spirits soar,
we're tied in imagination to what we know,
to the world of our senses and what they, alone, can tell us.
So we picture God's kingdom in terms of this one,
its beauty and blessings akin to those that surround us,
only writ more large.
True, there's enough in creation to move us to wonder,
to speak of God's love and purpose in astonishing ways,
but the joy he holds in store is greater than we can begin to imagine,
more special than words can express.
They asked their question, those Sadducees,
because they didn't believe resurrection was possible,
the idea of God sharing eternity with us
seeming utterly preposterous.
But far from proving the impossibility of everlasting life that day,
they demonstrated merely the limitations of the human mind.
Never confuse the two.

Quiet reflection

Prayer

Lord,
we find it hard to believe in resurrection sometimes,
for death seems so stark,
so final.
How can dust or ashes be brought back to life?
We struggle to take it in.
Remind us that some truths are beyond us;
that if we limit you to what we can fully understand
we will never believe,
for your ways are not our ways,
nor our thoughts your thoughts.

Open our hearts to things unseen,
and may our daily experience of your living presence
testify to the truth of what our minds cannot fathom:
the victory of your love.
Amen.

Silence

Comment

For even the most committed of us it's hard occasionally not to face doubts when confronted with the harsh realities of life, the trials and tragedies so many have to endure. We see famine, disease, war and natural disaster – hundreds of thousands sick, dying or living in abject poverty – and understandably we ask 'Why?' Where is God in all this? How can he allow it to continue? There are no easy answers to such questions, and we'll probably all approach them in different ways. One possibility is suggested by the following reading from the Gospel of Luke in which Jesus appears to speak of such things as being a necessary prelude to his coming again. What did he mean? And what does that mean for us today?

Music *(optional)*

Maranatha – come, Lord Jesus (Sacred Weave) Keith Duke

Reading

Luke 21:5-19

Meditation of a listener to Jesus

Wars?
Insurrections?
Earthquakes, famine and plague?
I thought Jesus came to bring an end to such things,

to make this a better world,
free from pain and sorrow.
But there he was talking as though these were part of God's plan,
necessary for the fulfilment of his purpose.
What was going on?
How did it fit together?
I wrestled with such questions for years afterwards,
the disasters and calamities of this world
more than once threatening my newfound faith,
but finally I understood.
God doesn't will such things –
they cut deep into his heart –
but there's no quick fix to spirit them away,
for they're part of the fabric of life,
integral to the world as we know it,
and unless we want him to destroy all that,
and us with it,
we must live with them as best we can.
There have always been wars,
always been catastrophes,
and so it will be until the time comes for a new heaven and earth,
when heartbreak and suffering will be no more.
Don't despair, then, in the trials and traumas of this world,
seeing in them reason to doubt his love.
See in them rather proof of how much we need him,
and keep faith, come what may,
that one day his will shall be done
and his kingdom come.

Quiet reflection

Prayer

We want to believe, Lord,
to trust in your purpose,
but we find it hard sometimes,
for so much seems to deny your love.

We see people broken by sickness, violence and disaster;
lives blighted by poverty and hunger;
a world scarred by greed, injustice and war;
and we wonder why you let it be.
Teach us that you not only feel our pain
but long to answer it;
that, however hard it is to see,
you are always at work,
seeking to bring good out of evil,
hope from despair,
life after death.
Help us, then,
however hard it may be,
to keep faith,
trusting that in the fullness of time your will shall be done
and your kingdom come.
Amen.

Silent retreat

Closing comment

It's often said we learn something new every day, and hopefully that's true, for as long as we're a part of this world we should never stop learning. It's part of being alive, part of what makes this world special, and it's part also of being a Christian, what faith is all about, for surely our knowledge and understanding of God should always be growing. As the Apostle Paul reminds us, in this life we see only a fraction of the whole. There is always more to discover, more to be revealed, more to know, and to unearth those hidden riches we need to ask questions and be open to being questioned in turn. We may not have all the answers, but of one thing we can be sure: *God does.*

Closing prayer

Mighty God,
help us to live with the mysteries of faith
and conundrums of life,
trusting always in you for help and guidance.
Keep us open to your searching voice,
ready to recognise your challenge and to respond.
Keep us eager to seek,
hungry to learn more
rather than closing our minds to what might stretch them.
Be with those who struggle with questions,
those who run from them,
and those who, through asking them, seek deeper insight and faith,
and lead all into a living knowledge of you,
through Jesus Christ our Lord.
Amen.

Amazing grace

Suggested visual material

Jesus of Nazareth 4 and 6
The Life of Christ II–III
Oberammergau 1990

FIRST SESSION

Introduction

A stern judge passing sentence: we know it's entirely the wrong picture, but we find it hard to escape from that perception of God. Perhaps it reflects the influence of the Old Testament, which though it undoubtedly contains many wonderful images of God as gentle and full of mercy, has a lot to say as well about his anger, jealousy, even vindictiveness. Maybe we also find it hard to escape from an innate sense of guilt, not stemming from any shocking wrongdoing but simply from those little faults and failings which, taken together, can be so destructive of both ourselves and others. Whatever the reason, we can lose sight of the God presented in the Gospels and encountered above all in the person of Jesus: the God who refuses to condemn, who continues to love despite betrayal, denial and rejection; who delights to forgive and forget, asking only that we come to him in genuine repentance and resolved to start again. Faith, despite the way we sometimes present it, is about mercy, not punishment; about wiping the slate clean rather than being held to account. Today, through readings and meditations, we're going to remind ourselves of that truth and explore what it means so that we shall more fully celebrate the wonder of what God has done and wants yet to do for all.

Opening prayer

Sovereign God,
we come to you in awe,
but also in assurance;
in humility,
but also in quiet confidence.
We come, not with fear and trembling,
but gladly,
knowing your way is to bless instead of curse,
forgive instead of punish,
heal instead of hurt.
Though we fail you,
still you love us;
though *we* prove false,
always *you* stay true;
your mercy being far wider than our own,
defying our understanding.
So now we pray, once more:
pardon our shortcomings
cleanse us of our faults,
and help us to greet each day with gratitude,
celebrating the freedom you so graciously offer
and showing a similar generosity of spirit in all our dealings with others.
Amen.

Comment

'There's no such thing as a free lunch,' we're often told. Or again: 'You don't get something for nothing.' Such is the received wisdom of our world. And it's sentiments like those that make it so hard for us to grasp the full extent of God's mercy. Unconditional mercy seems counterintuitive, contradicting our sense of fair play. Debts, after all, have to be paid, mistakes put right, wrongs atoned for. And in terms of earthly justice that's true, or else anarchy would swiftly follow. But God's ways are not ours. If he applied such criteria there would be no hope for any of us. The attitude of Simon the Pharisee in the following reading typifies our way of looking at things; that of Jesus exemplifies God's.

Music *(optional)*

Jesus, you are the way (Fountain of Life) Margaret Rizza

Reading

Luke 7:36–8:3

Meditation of Simon, the Pharisee

Debt cancelled?
Sins forgiven?
What sort of talk is that?
We've rules for such things,
criteria set out in the Law,
and these people Jesus so freely mixes with
fall short of them by a mile,
wholly undeserving of pardon.
He should know that, *surely*,
for he's no fool,
yet he not only speaks of mercy
but seems to think *he* has the right to grant it.
Preposterous!
I challenged him, of course,
and he came up then with some hypothetical story
intended to put me on the spot.
But it wasn't *me* who needed to judge rightly;
it was *him*.
Those in debt should expect to pay off what they owe,
that's how I saw it,
and the same applies with wrongdoing.
You can't just go round excusing mistakes,
writing them off as though they never happened.
A price must be paid –
and if the guilty party won't pay it, then *who will*?
No, he means well, I'm sure,
but he's out of touch with the world,
the way people really are.

Give them an inch and they'll take a mile.
I'm all for forgiveness, don't get me wrong,
but there needs to be change to back it up,
transformation deep within,
and it would take something very special to happen to achieve that,
don't you think?
Something, or some*one*, altogether unique!

Quiet reflection

Prayer

Thank you, Lord, that you came not to judge
but to acquit,
not to condemn
but to pardon.
Thank you for seeing us as we are,
with all our faults and weaknesses,
yet loving us just the same
and refusing to write us off.
Teach us, in turn, to see the good in others
and in whatever we can to help bring out their best.
Amen.

Silence

Comment

The parable of the lost coin is one of the best loved in the New Testament – refreshingly homely, wonderfully easy to understand, yet graphically putting across God's unfailing love and patience. We accept its message of forgiveness readily enough in principle, but how far do we apply it to ourselves, and how far equally to others? Listen again and marvel at the implications of this memorable story.

Music *(optional)*

O give thanks to the Lord (Light in our Darkness) Margaret Rizza

Reading

Luke 15:1-10

Meditation of a scribe

He's right, you know,
in one thing at least.
I dropped a coin myself the other day,
just one denarius, worth next to nothing,
yet I hunted around on my hands and knees for hours
until at last I found it.
That was *money* though.
It's different with people,
not least because they *choose* to be lost
and can choose to be found.
Don't give me any of that sob-story stuff.
They know the score,
what's right and wrong;
it's spelt out clearly enough in the commandments,
and if they decide to ignore those
then they'll get what's coming to them.
Oh, they can make amends . . . in theory –
accept their punishment and start again –
but can you see any of them changing their spots?
I can't.
No, some people are beyond the pale,
irredeemable.
Yet there was Jesus
mixing with undesirables without even a hint of shame,
suggesting *God* had time for them even if *we* didn't.
He means well, I'm sure,
but he's so gullible,
so naïve,

really seeming to believe that all it takes to receive God's pardon
is to be truly sorry.
What does he think heaven is: open to *everyone*,
entered not on merit but through God's grace?
A right motley bunch we'd find there then!
I tell you what,
if he's right, you won't find me there, that's for sure . . .
What's that?
Couldn't have put it better yourself?
Choosing to be lost?
Now hang on a minute!

Quiet reflection

Prayer

Thank you, Lord, that when we go astray,
you seek us out,
searching until you find;
that whatever our mistakes,
and however often we fail,
still you come looking for us,
each of us precious in your eyes.
Help us to recognise the enormity of your love
and extent of your mercy;
to receive the forgiveness you so freely offer
and, by your grace, to start again,
restored,
redeemed,
renewed.
Amen.

Silent retreat

SECOND SESSION

Comment

If there's a danger of understating God's mercy, paradoxically there's a risk also of failing to recognise our need of it. We all have our blind spots, weaknesses that have become so much a part of us that we're the last to see them, and it's those rather than the faults we're aware of that should concern us. They can lead us into the trap of thinking that, compared to others, there's not so much wrong in our lives after all; even that we deserve God's blessing. Hypocrisy and holier-than-thou attitudes are fallen into more easily than we might imagine. Our next reading warns against such misplaced confidence, reminding us that forgiveness is dependent entirely on God's grace, never on our own merits.

Music *(optional)*

Miserere mei Allegri

Reading

Luke 18:9-14

Meditation of a listener to the parable of the Pharisee and the tax-collector

Was it even a prayer, that cry of the tax-collector?
Think about it:
he refused to approach God,
wouldn't even look towards heaven
so great was his sense of unworthiness –
his utter guilt and shame.
Don't ask me what sin he was meant to have committed,
but it was clearly nothing to be proud of,
and the fellow knew it.
The Pharisee, by contrast, may have been a touch self-righteous,
smug even,

but give him his due,
he'd have observed the Law to the letter,
scrupulous in every detail.
Can you really ask for more than that?
Tell me, which of the two would you have kept company with,
given the choice?
Which would you have trusted with your money,
your children,
your life?
Do I need to ask?
No, the Pharisees have their faults, certainly,
but they're devout,
upright,
God-fearing –
decent and respectable folk like you and me.
So what was Jesus thinking of, telling a story like that?
Honestly, he'll give religion a bad name with such talk,
as if all our dutiful devotion can somehow be worth less
than a single cry from the heart.
Surely not even *he* can mean that!
Can he?

Quiet reflection

Prayer

Lord Jesus Christ, forgive us,
for we fail you time and again,
betraying and denying your love.
We are weak, stubborn, proud, foolish,
false and faithless in so much.
Cleanse us from our faults
for they are ever before us.
Have mercy, Lord,
have mercy upon us all.
Amen.

Silence

Comment

Is saying sorry enough in itself to secure forgiveness? It's a question that leads us back to the old chestnut of how faith relates to works; whether we're justified by faith alone or by deeds as well. The exact relationship between the two has taxed the intellects of untold generations, yet the well-loved story of our reading surely leaves us in no doubt. Genuine sorrow is sufficient, but it should necessarily express itself in a desire to change. In other words, if it's the real thing, repentance should *show*. That's not to say we'll become whiter than white overnight or even that, in the long run, we'll change at all, despite our best intentions, but intentions should be there nonetheless, as also should actions, just as they so clearly were for Zacchaeus.

Music *(optional)*

Have mercy on us, Lord (In God Alone) Andrew Moore

Reading

Luke 19:1-10

Meditation of Zacchaeus

It wasn't enough simply to say sorry –
to admit that I'd made mistakes.
Words come cheap, don't they? –
eventually counting for nothing, however fine they seem.
I needed to do more,
to show that I *meant* what I *said*,
and so,
there and then,
I offered half of my possessions to the poor,
and promised to repay any I'd defrauded:
not just what I owed them
but four times as much again.

Generous you think?
Impulsive?
Even over the top?
Perhaps,
but it was as nothing compared to the riches I'd found in Jesus,
the joy of being loved and accepted as I was
and allowed to start again.
I'd have sacrificed anything for that,
and here it was being offered to me for free:
nothing demanded,
nothing expected –
simply held out to receive.
I could never repay such a gift,
still less earn it,
and it didn't occur to me to try.
That gesture of mine was not a making amends or settling the debt,
but a way of saying thank you and sorry rolled into one:
of expressing what I felt, not just in words,
but in deeds.

Quiet reflection

Prayer

Forgive us, Lord,
for too often we say sorry to you and others,
but don't really mean it,
our lives giving the lie to our words.
Though we cannot earn forgiveness,
still less deserve it,
help us to show the sincerity of our repentance
through a real desire to change;
to express our gratitude for your unfailing mercy
whenever and wherever we can.
Amen.

Silent retreat

Closing comment

Recognising our *need* for forgiveness, *accepting* forgiveness, *celebrating* forgiveness, offering forgiveness to *others*: put those together and we get very close to a summary of what the gospel is all about. How is it that Christian faith has come to be seen by many as morbidly preoccupied with sin and guilt? How is it that the Church is associated in the eyes of some with intolerance, self-righteousness, narrow and judgemental attitudes? All these are the very antithesis of what should be the case. If we live by the grace of Christ, rejoicing in the freedom he makes possible, then who and what we are will speak of inner peace, love and acceptance. We cannot answer for others, or for the way some will invariably misjudge us, seeing only what they want to see, but we *can* answer for the message *we* put across, whether we live, as best we can and with Christ's help, according to the credo of forgiveness. Do that, and we won't go far wrong.

Closing prayer

We return, Lord, to the daily round of life,
assured of your pardon.
thankful for the chance to start again,
resolved to live changed lives,
determined to express our gratitude
and eager to show mercy to others in turn.
Keep that flame burning within us,
that confidence strong and determination real,
so that we may truly live as your people,
redeemed,
restored,
renewed,
refashioned,
our lives testifying unmistakably to your gracious love.
Amen.

Who is this man?

Suggested visual material

Jesus, the Child
Jesus of Nazareth 1–6
The Life of Christ I–IV

FIRST SESSION

Introduction

Who can this man be? Time and again throughout his ministry, Jesus' words and deeds prompted that question, his teaching, his acts of healing, his whole way of life causing people to scratch their heads in a mixture of wonder and confusion. No ordinary man, surely, could do such things; no mere carpenter's son could speak with such authority; yet those who met him could see he was flesh and blood just as they were, so how did it all add up? Was he sent by God, as he seemed to claim? Was he the Messiah, promised of old? Was he even perhaps the Son of God, as his words appeared to suggest? These were profound and controversial questions, polarising public opinion and driving a wedge between people of one view or the other, dividing even family and friends. Such was the impact of this man and the nature of his ministry that few could ignore him.

What of us? We may think we've understood the truth, that we've made up our minds and made our commitment, but have we really grasped who Jesus is and what he means? Does what we say about him show itself in the way we live? Do we follow him in practice or in name alone? Today, through readings and reflections, we remind ourselves of the contrasting reception accorded to Jesus; the love he inspired in some and the hatred in others. As you listen and ponder, meet him again, greet him again, and respond again to this most extraordinary man.

Opening prayer

Saviour Christ
we proclaim you as Lord,
but fail to serve you as we should;
we acclaim you as King of kings,
yet our allegiance is hopelessly fickle.
In innumerable ways we deny in our lives
what we say with our lips,
our lack of love, trust, joy and peace
making a mockery of the faith we profess in you.
We hear your voice,
yet we ignore it.
We recognise your call,
but water it down.
Our commitment is half-hearted,
a shadow of what it could and should be,
more about what we would *like* you to be
than who you really are.
Forgive us,
and help us to know you better.
Deepen our understanding of your purpose,
our grasp of your grace,
so that we may honour you more fully,
love you more sincerely
and serve you more faithfully,
to the glory of your name.
Amen.

Comment

It wasn't only during the years of his ministry that Jesus excited comment. At the very beginning, shepherds and magi kneeled in wonder and went on their way rejoicing, and then, as the next reading and meditation reminds us, when he was but a boy he once again set the crowds talking, discussing among themselves just who he could be.

Music *(optional)*

Lovely in your littleness (Chants and Songs) Margaret Rizza

Reading

Luke 2:41-52

Meditation of a rabbi in the Jerusalem Temple

Who was this boy, we wondered –
so discerning,
so deep,
so mature for his years?
He wasn't your everyday youngster, that's for sure,
having instead an aura about him
unlike anything I've encountered before.
And those questions he asked:
astonishing! –
time and again making us scratch our heads not just in wonder
but in bewilderment,
for he brought out truths from the Scriptures
that we'd scarcely considered
and came up with answers to conundrums
that had foxed us for years.
It was uncanny,
unnerving,
almost as though he could read God's mind,
but, of course, it's blasphemy even to think that,
let alone to say it out loud.
He'd have had to be God's Son for that,
the promised Messiah,
and clearly he wasn't,
for suddenly his parents arrived,
all of a panic,
scolding the lad for having wandered off and got himself lost.
It's strange though,
for *we* were the assumed experts in the Law,

yet that whippersnapper taught us a thing or two that day,
making God real in a way we all secretly longed to emulate.
And there's something else, more puzzling still,
for when that couple turned up to collect him
he seemed surprised they were worried,
saying they should have known to look in his father's house,
almost as though it were here in the Temple,
among the things of God,
that he felt most at home.
Am I missing something?

Quiet reflection

Prayer

Lord Jesus Christ,
thank you for revealing the Father,
not just speaking his word
but coming among us,
walking our earth,
sharing our flesh and blood,
to make known his glory, greatness, power and purpose.
Thank you for giving God a human face,
one we can understand and relate to intimately –
making his love real.
Draw us closer to you
and so closer to him.
Amen.

Silence

Comment

As we're well aware, not everyone is ready to respond to Jesus, many having made up their minds about him without even considering his claims. Today that's probably more true than ever, the general assumption being that Christianity has been tried and found wanting, well intentioned perhaps but irrelevant to our modern age. Not that closed minds are anything new. Our next reading and reflection remind us that Jesus faced such rejection from the very start of his ministry.

Music *(optional)*

All you nations (Awakening in Love) Margaret Rizza

Reading

Luke 4:14-21

Meditation of a member of the synagogue in Nazareth

We knew what he was going to say,
even before he said it,
and if at first we'd been filled with pride
delighted to hear one of our own read so beautifully,
in a trice it all changed,
our mood turning to anger at the sheer presumption of the man.
There had been a note of challenge in his voice from the start,
as though he believed those words of Isaiah referred directly to him
and dare we suggest otherwise.
So when he returned the scroll and sat back down,
our eyes never left his,
nor his ours.
It was like a battle of wills,
a test of strength:
who would declare their hand first?
Eventually, it was Jesus who broke the silence,
confirming our worst suspicions.
'Today,' he said, 'this scripture has been fulfilled in your hearing,'
implying it was somehow fulfilled in him!
What rubbish!
We knew who this man was,
having seen him grow up among us,

suckle at his mother's breast,
labour in his father's workshop –
he was just an ordinary person like you and me.
So what gave him the right to put on such airs and graces?
Okay, so he'd caused a stir in the surrounding villages
with a few signs and wonders,
and maybe he did know the Scriptures better than the rest of us,
but that didn't make him God's gift, did it!
He came up then with some fancy line,
suggesting a prophet is without honour in his own country,
as though that somehow proved his point.
But it didn't, not to my mind,
for he was making himself out to be much more than that:
the fulfilment of God's promises of old.
No, we'd have recognised a prophet all right,
but for him to be who he said he was,
sent and anointed by God,
he'd have had to be someone far greater –
the promised Messiah,
Son of God –
and, in all honesty, could anyone miss that?!

Quiet reflection

Prayer

Open our eyes, Lord, to the good in those around us,
those we know so well that we can sometimes take them for granted.
Help us to recognise their gifts,
their qualities,
their contribution to our lives,
and to encourage them through genuine appreciation
of all that they do and are.
Amen.

Silence

Comment

One of the most mysterious and enigmatic events recorded in the Gospels is the so-called transfiguration of Jesus; that moment on the mountaintop when he seemed to be transformed before Peter, James and John so that they stood there open-mouthed, lost for words, rubbing their eyes in disbelief. What actually happened there we can't be sure, but the result was that the way those three apostles perceived Jesus was never the same again. They realised, albeit still partially, that he was more than just a man, greater than they'd begun to contemplate. It was an experience that stretched their horizons and deepened their faith; one of many that were to do the same. For us too, faith and understanding should always be growing. However much we love Jesus, however much we may think we know of him, there is always more yet to be revealed.

Music *(optional)*

O Magnum Mysterium Palestrina

Reading

Luke 9:28-36

Meditation of the Apostle James

We thought we knew him,
that we understood who he was
and what he'd come to do.
We'd followed him for months, remember,
walked and talked with him like no other,
so all of us, in our own way, understood he was special,
chosen and called by God.
We believed he was the Messiah,
come to set us free –
the one sent by God to establish his kingdom here on earth,
a glorious new beginning.

Never mind the whys and wherefores –
they could wait.
He was here among us,
working out his purpose,
and that was enough.
But we *didn't* really know, after all,
as that day on the mountaintop made clear,
our horizons exposed there as painfully small,
altogether lacking.
For in those extraordinary few moments
we glimpsed him as never before:
bathed in the glory of God,
transformed,
radiant,
not of this world.
And, as if to confirm how unique he was,
a voice came from heaven:
'This is my Son . . .
listen to him.'
We realised then that he didn't just *speak* of God –
he *was* God,
greater than we'd begun to imagine,
than words can ever express –
the cloud that overshadowed us a reminder that we saw but in part,
gazed upon a mighty and marvellous mystery.
We had much to learn,
and we're learning still,
day after day discovering more of his grace,
his love,
his truth.
Never forget the lesson we were given:
that whatever we know of who and what he is,
there will always be far, far more beyond us.

Quiet reflection

Prayer

Lord Jesus Christ,
we think we know you,
imagine we have understood who and what you are,
but in reality we have barely glimpsed your glory,
scarcely begun to grasp the extent of your power,
scope of your purpose,
breadth of your love
or depth of your mercy.
Remind us that true faith is always growing,
never the finished article;
that we have more to learn,
more to discover,
more to experience of your grace and goodness.
Help us to recognise a little more of your greatness each day,
until we finally see and know you in full,
even as we are fully known.
Amen.

Silence

Comment

Should religion divide people? No, or at least not in the sense of rejecting those who think differently from us, arguing over points of doctrine, or persecuting people for their faith or lack of it. But that's not to say it won't cause disagreement, because of course, by its very nature, it will. Jesus made huge and astonishing claims for himself, and issued equally bold challenges, calling us to changed lives, to deciding for or against him, to continuing on our own way or walking in his. Understandably some find that hard, and it's not for us to condemn or force our beliefs upon them; our job is simply through word and deed to share our faith as honestly and lovingly as possible. We cannot answer for others; only for ourselves.

Music *(optional)*

Exaudi nos, Domine (Chants and Songs) Margaret Rizza

Reading

Luke 7:11-17

Meditation of the widow whose son was raised by Jesus

'Do not weep,' he urged,
and I could hardly believe my ears,
for it seemed such a stupid, senseless thing to say.
My son had just died, remember –
my one and only son! –
and I was desolate,
distraught,
beside myself with grief.
My world had turned to dust,
and here was this stranger popping up out of nowhere
and telling me not to cry –
as though I should pull myself together,
be stronger,
take it on the chin.
I tell you, I wanted to knock his block off,
but I'd neither the strength
nor the spirit,
my only thought being to bury the poor lad
and then curl up at home in a corner
and sob my heart out.
Yet still Jesus stood there before me,
and I caught something in his gaze –
a look of gentle authority such as I'd never seen before –
that made my stomach lurch within me,
inexplicably stirred by hope.
And then he turned to where my son was lying,
and spoke to him,
softly and simply:
'Young man . . . rise.'
We watched, incredulous,
held like those in a trance,
unable to believe what our eyes were telling us
yet unable, equally, to deny what we saw.

He was alive again –
my child who had lain there moments before so still and cold –
living and breathing once more,
hugging me in his warm embrace,
dancing for joy.
Well, you can imagine the celebrations –
what a party we had! –
and though some tried afterwards to explain it all away,
suggesting that the boy, perhaps, hadn't been quite dead,
merely lying in a coma,
I knew different,
beyond a shadow of doubt.
He'd been taken from me,
and given back;
he'd passed away,
and then returned;
and suddenly I found myself recalling other words of Jesus,
spoken long before;
then a mystery
but now so wonderfully clear:
'Blessed are those who mourn,
for they will be comforted.'
I believe that, you know,
totally,
without reserve,
for Jesus has shown me that, by God's grace,
even death can be defeated.
Life may be snuffed out,
seemingly for ever,
bringing pain, horror, heartbreak,
but it's not the end,
simply the path to a new beginning,
for his love is stronger than all.

Quiet reflection

Prayer

To all, Lord, who walk in the shadow of death,
speak your word of hope and promise.
Reach out to those who have lost loved ones,
and to those who are terminally ill;
those overwhelmed by sorrow
and those wrestling with fear
as they come to terms with their own mortality.
Grant to all who mourn real and lasting comfort,
both through the knowledge of your presence with them now
and through the assurance of life to come.
May they and we know, even in the midst of tears and heartache,
that there is nothing in heaven or earth,
life or death,
that will ever be able to separate us from your love
which is ours through Jesus Christ our Lord.
Amen.

Silent retreat

SECOND SESSION

Comment

How do you show something to be true? Simply by insisting that you're right? Or by demonstrating the truth in practice? The latter, as any teacher will know, is by far the most effective. When we've worked something out for ourselves, made sense of it firsthand, it means far more to us than a lesson learnt parrot fashion. But, of course, before we can accept the truth of anything we must first be open to it, willing to weigh up the evidence before us. The importance of both those factors is spelt out clearly in the following reading and reflection. As Jesus put it: do we have eyes to see and ears to hear?

Music *(optional)*

Lift up your heads, O ye gates (Messiah) Handel

Reading

John 10:22-30

Meditation of a Sadducee listening to Jesus

Why didn't he tell us who he was?
Why beat about the bush,
talking in parables and riddles,
when he could have made things clear?
Was he the Messiah or wasn't he?
But he wouldn't come clean,
seeming determined instead to keep us guessing.
Well, what could we make of that?
It seemed obvious he wasn't the Messiah after all,
but that he wanted us to think he *might* be;
that, despite all his claims to the contrary,
he enjoyed the mystique,
the attentions of the crowd,
and wanted to keep it going.
Even then, though, we wanted to believe,
hoping we might be wrong,
so we put him on the spot,
asking him to give it to us straight,
one way or the other.
And what did he talk about in reply?
Sheep!
I know: extraordinary, isn't it!
He seemed to imply we had only to listen
and the truth would be revealed,
but that we'd made up our minds already
and were resolved *not* to hear.
What nonsense!
The truth is that, for all his signs and wonders,
God's reign on earth seemed as far away as ever,
consigned to some future kingdom
rather than established here today.
Well I'm sorry, but we don't go in for all that pie-in-the-sky nonsense,
resurrection and eternal life,

and we never will
unless someone comes back from the dead to prove it.
Let Jesus do that and we'll revise our opinion,
of him and everything,
for *of course* we'll believe then –
who wouldn't?
But I don't think that's likely.
Do *you*?

Prayer

Living Lord,
in a sceptical and cynical world that refuses to believe,
help us to keep faith in you.
Though we cannot prove you rose again,
or that *we* will either,
may your voice continue to ring true within us,
speaking of your risen presence and promise of life –
a sure and certain hope.
Amen.

Quiet reflection

Comment

We were reminded earlier of the transfiguration and how it led some of the apostles to a deeper understanding of Christ's glory and power. Our next reading speaks of a very different experience, yet one which in its own way would again have stretched their understanding of who Jesus was and what he came to do. Like the rest of Israel, they were anticipating still a messiah who would set them free from Roman oppression and establish an earthly kingdom with himself on the throne. Instead, the truth began to dawn that Jesus came to rule through serving others; to be raised up through being brought low; to be first through being last.

Music *(optional)*

He was despised and rejected (Messiah) Handel

Reading

John 13:1-17, 31b-35

Meditation of Simon Peter

Would *you* have washed my feet?
I wouldn't have done, in his place,
for they were dirty,
sweaty,
smelly,
so when Jesus came round to me with that bowl and towel,
well, there's no other word for it,
I was mortified!
He was the teacher,
I the pupil;
he the Lord,
me a mere disciple,
so what was he thinking of,
demeaning himself like that,
as though I were the master
and he the slave?!
He was right though:
I *did* understand later.
After they'd whipped him,
struck him,
abused him,
killed him,
everything became clear.
Finally, *finally*, it got through to me:
that the last will be first and the least greatest;
that those who lose their life will find it;
that the humble will be lifted up and the proud brought low.
I needed to learn those values of his kingdom,

so different,
so contrary to our own,
and that night,
as he stooped before me,
was another lesson in love.
He humbled himself,
in life and in death,
a servant to us all.
Will you serve *him* in turn?

Quiet reflection

Prayer

In a self-serving world, Lord,
where greed rules,
profit is everything
and looking after number one is the all-consuming creed,
teach us your way:
the way of humility, sacrifice and service.
Give us the love and courage we need
not just to learn of it
but to put it into practice;
to take up our cross
and follow you.
Amen.

Silence

Comment

What must Mary, mother of Jesus, have gone through as she watched her son suffer and die on the cross? Had she grasped by then just who he was? Did she understand why he so willingly surrendered his life? Who can say? But witnessing there the depth of his love – both for herself and for others – must have brought home to her in a way nothing else could have begun to just how unique he was. She'd known from the beginning he was sent by God. As Jesus breathed his last, could she understand why?

Music *(optional)*

Ave Maria Gounod

Readings

Luke 2:33-35; John 19:25-27

Meditation of Mary, mother of Jesus

I was so proud,
so happy as I held our child close,
cradling him in my arms.
He seemed more special,
more precious,
than I'd dreamt possible,
and I wept tears of joy.
But just days later,
a shadow fell that was never quite to lift,
for that man Simeon, as we took Jesus to the Temple,
warned of hurt,
heartbreak,
a sword piercing my soul.
And now, all this time later,
after years of wondering,
hoping he might be wrong,
I've come, all too clearly, to see what he meant.
For it's my boy up there, hanging on that cross;
it's my boy, grimacing with pain;
it's my boy, broken and bleeding;
it's my boy, breathing his last –
and no words can express my pain.
He brought it on himself, in a sense,
choosing the way of the cross,

and though I'd begged him to think again,
I'd known all along, in my heart of hearts,
that there was no other way –
that he had to fulfil his calling.
My heart ached with pride,
even while it groaned with grief,
and if, earlier, joy had been touched with sorrow,
now sorrow was touched with joy,
for even as he writhed there in agony,
he looked down at me
and showed how much he cared,
asking John,
his dearest, closest friend,
to look after me –
treat me like a mum.
I had to let go of my child,
just as we all do,
his life having brought me pleasure and pain,
laughter and tears.
But, whatever the cost, it was worth it,
a thousand times over,
for through him, I've been truly blessed,
and so also, if you've only eyes to see it, have *you*.

Quiet reflection

Prayer

For the wonder of your love, Lord,
poured out for many;
for the immensity of your sacrifice,
offered for all;
for the depth of your care,
never exhausted;
for the richness of your blessing,
so freely given;
from the bottom of our hearts, we thank you.
Amen.

Silence

Comment

An incredible teacher, a truly extraordinary man – many are willing to admit that of Jesus. But is it enough? Does it get anywhere near to expressing the truth of who he was, the wonder of what he did, the awesomeness of what he continues to do? For the Christian, the answer is a resounding no. A great teacher and amazing man he most certainly was, but such descriptions barely scratch the surface of his nature, his purpose, his love, his being. Though we struggle to get our heads round it, we believe he is with us now through his Spirit, yet also enthroned on high – *from* God, *with* God, *of* God – human yet divine. However much we reflect on who he is, we can never exhaust the mystery of his greatness of which we still have so much to learn.

Music *(optional)*

The Mirror of the Trinity (Magnificat) Praetorius

Reading

John 16:12-15

Meditation of the Apostle John

He's done the impossible,
putting us right with God –
not through any deserving on our part,
but simply and solely through his grace,
his costly redeeming love.
The debt is cancelled,
barrier broken,
chasm between us bridged –
we are at one with the Father,
reconciled in Christ.
But if *that* seems amazing,
there's more still,

for our friend Jesus –
who walked our earth
and died our death –
is not just *at one* with God;
he *is* one.
It doesn't make sense, does it?
But it's true nonetheless,
for he's shown us the Father,
just as he said he would –
God's love and purpose revealed in the Word made flesh.
And if that's not enough,
Christ is here now,
working within us through his Spirit,
day after day energising,
teaching,
guiding,
empowering –
seeking to make us new.
Father, Son and Holy Spirit:
they don't just *point* to each other,
they *are* each other . . .
and yet they're not,
for each also is distinct,
the three, one,
yet the one, three.
Yes, I know what you're thinking –
'That really *is* impossible!' –
and I know just how you feel,
but I know something else as well,
proven by experience across the years.
Impossible or not,
it's also true!

Prayer

Lord Jesus Christ,
Son of God,
thank you for helping us to know the Father,
to glimpse his face,

hear his voice,
see his glory.
Lord Jesus Christ,
the Word made flesh,
thank you for making God real,
present among us,
sharing our humanity,
identifying with us in life and death,
and opening the way to your kingdom.
Lord Jesus Christ,
giver of life,
thank you for your Holy Spirit,
constantly at work,
in our lives,
in your Church,
in the world.
Living Lord,
we offer our thanks,
we give you our praise,
we pledge you our service.
Amen.

Silent retreat

Closing comment

We've heard what others have thought of Jesus – the questions they asked and conclusions they drew – and each has something to teach us in our own journey of faith, but eventually, of course, it's not what others think that's important; it's what *we* think. Remember how Jesus, while walking with his disciples, asked them first 'Who do people say that I am?' After they answered him that, he turned to them again, posing the all-important question: 'And what about you; who do *you* say that I am?' No one else can answer that for us. We must decide for ourselves. Are we for or against him? Do we accept or reject his claims? Have we decided he's not who he claims to be, or are we ready to believe, trust and follow, wherever he might lead?

Closing prayer

Lord Jesus Christ,
by your grace keep our relationship with you real,
immediate,
and personal –
not based on what others have told us,
or on what we once felt but feel no longer,
but rooted in an ongoing experience of your love,
a daily walking with you,
an awareness of your constant grace and goodness.
Save us from nominal commitment or borrowed faith,
a life that has lost touch with you.
Draw near each day
and keep us close.
Amen.

The way of Christ

Suggested visual material

Jesus of Nazareth 2–4
The Life of Christ II

FIRST SESSION

Introduction

It's easy to call oneself a Christian. Thousands do so up and down the country, yet have little if any idea what it really means, the term serving as merely a label for nominal belief. Interestingly, early believers in Jesus were known simply as followers of the way, and few descriptions take us more succinctly yet eloquently to the heart of what being a Christian is all about. It involves a journey of discipleship, committing ourselves as best we're able to walking in the footsteps of Christ. It means seeking to emulate his example; taking the path of love, compassion, obedience and commitment; seeking God's will and putting the good of others before our own. Do we still have that perspective on faith? Do we see ourselves as a pilgrim people, travelling the Christian road? Or have we started to wander round in circles; even perhaps ground to a halt or slipped backwards? And, if so, why? Today, through readings and reflections, and, above all, through silence, let us consider afresh the call of Christ, and what it means to walk his way.

Opening prayer

Almighty God,
we praise you for your love, grace and goodness revealed in Christ,
for your having shared our humanity through him,
experiencing firsthand our joys and sorrows,
hopes and fears.

As we reflect today on the path of his ministry
and his faithfulness to your call,
equip and inspire us to walk his way in turn.
Renew our faith,
restore our vision
and renew our commitment,
so that we may live and work for him,
matching our footsteps to his until our journey's end.
Amen.

Comment

Leading a distinctive lifestyle is not easy, for in a host of ways we are all faced with pressure to conform. And that is especially so if the lifestyle we choose runs counter to the accepted norms of the world, challenging people's assumptions and preconceptions. So it was for Jesus, to the point that some questioned his sanity, others attempted to smear him, and others again made attempts on his life – anything to deflect attention away from his message. Even his own family succumbed to the temptation to distance themselves from what he said, urging him to go easy, to bend a little rather than get people's backs up. For Jesus, staying true to his calling meant sacrifice long before it led to a cross. It meant enduring rejection and hostility, choosing between popular acclaim and divine approval. He had to look beyond ties of family and friends if he were to walk the way God asked of him. Do we have similar courage to follow in turn?

Music *(optional)*

We come (Across the Water) Keith Duke

Reading

Mark 3:20-35

Meditation of Mary, mother of Jesus

Were we upset by his response,
by his ignoring us in favour of the crowd?
Not a bit of it.
We were ashamed more like,
for we should have known better than to pressure him as we did.
We tried to restrain him, you know –
told him to make haste slowly,
avoid causing offence –
and all because some people were saying,
'He has gone out of his mind.'
They were shocked, I suppose,
by his challenging the authority of the Pharisees,
interpreting the Law,
and setting himself up as a teacher, with disciples in tow.
But, of course, they shouldn't have been,
for that's what God had called him to do,
why he'd come into the world,
as they'd surely have understood if they'd only listened.
How could we care more about what *they* thought than about him?
But, foolishly,
we did.
The crowd didn't though –
those gathered around him when we arrived.
They were drinking in his every word,
listening with rapt attention,
wonder in their eyes.
Never mind what others said –
to them he was special,
making God known in a way no one had done before.
All right, so blood may be thicker than water,
but at that moment *they* were being his family,
not *us*,
for they were honouring the Father,
doing his will.
That's what he wants from us –
from you,

from me,
from everyone.
That's what it means to be his people:
to love and serve God.
I forgot that for a moment,
and was rightly reproached.
May he save me from making the same mistake again.

Quiet reflection

Prayer

Lord Jesus Christ,
thank you for staying true to us despite the cost,
for walking the way of love
even though it was also the way of the cross.
Help us to stay true in turn,
not being swayed by what others say of you,
by the response of this world,
but proving our commitment through honouring the Father,
seeking to do his will.
Teach us that if we would truly do that,
we must be one with you,
equipped and enabled by your grace to follow in your footsteps
as best we can.
Amen.

Silence

Comment

What, then, are the qualities that mark the way of Christ? For Jesus, the answer could be seen in a little child, as is so clearly illustrated in his celebrated welcoming of the children brought to him to touch, and his rebuke of the disciples for attempting to turn them away. Instead of offering us a definitive list, he invites us to explore the characteristics of childhood that we need to retain in our journey of faith. They include such qualities as trust, humility, an enquiring mind, a sense of wonder, an openness to new ideas, and a hunger to grow. Do we have those childlike attributes, so necessary to faithful discipleship, and, if not, are we ready to seek them out once more?

Music *(optional)*

Jeux d'enfants (Petite Suite) Bizet

Reading

Mark 10:2-16

Meditation of those who brought their children to Jesus

1 He took our children in his arms,
welcoming them with a smile on his lips
and warmth in his eyes,
but had it been up to those disciples of his,
none of us would have got anywhere near him,
for they brusquely shooed us away.
2 Don't distract him, was the message.
Can't you see the Master's busy;
that he's got better things to do with his time than fritter it away
on doting mothers and their soppy kids?
3 And, were it not for Jesus, we'd have gone home,
disappointed,
angry,
but resigned.
1 He, though, was more indignant than *any* of us,
reprimanding his followers as though *they* were the children.
And then he turned to our little ones,
all attention,
as though nothing in the world could matter to him more.
3 And, do you know what? – I actually think that's true.
They were special to *him*, that much was obvious,
but he reckoned also they were special to *God*,
the kingdom of heaven somehow theirs.

2 We were flabbergasted at that,
for we'd a sneaking feeling the disciples were right –
that faith's not kids' stuff,
but difficult,
demanding,
hard to understand.
3 It's not, though.
It's incredibly simple –
about responding to love,
receiving a gift,
accepting a welcome.
1 *We're* the ones who complicate it,
not God.
We burden others with heavy loads
and tie ourselves in knots,
when he longs only to set us free.
2 Don't try to work it out.
Don't get bogged down in the details.
Receive the kingdom, he said, as a little child
or you may never enter it at all.

Quiet reflection

Prayer

Gracious God,
thank you for accepting us into the family of your people –
for welcoming us, not as slaves or servants,
but as your children,
precious to you.
Teach us what that means,
and help us always to retain a youthful faith,
fresh,
trusting,
enthusiastic –
not childish
but childlike,
full of hope and anticipation.

Give us innocence and humility
to accept that we depend ultimately on you,
and that, however long we've been walking the way of Christ,
we've still only just begun.
Amen.

Silent retreat

SECOND SESSION

Comment

We've touched already on the costly commitment of Jesus, the fact that his way involved suffering, even to the point of death. But, of course, it meant cost not just to himself but to those who followed in his footsteps. Many of the apostles, for example, endured fierce persecution, some likewise making the ultimate sacrifice for his sake, and so it has been for countless of his followers in the years since. Happily, so high a price is asked of few of us today, but true commitment can still ask much of us in various ways. It can lead to mockery and misunderstanding, hostility and indifference, rejection and opposition. Are we willing to walk the way that puts God and others before ourselves?

Music *(optional)*

The traveller (Across the Water) Keith Duke

Reading

Mark 10:17-31

Meditation of Simon Peter

It seemed natural at first,
not just the right thing to do, but the *only* thing.
He called,

and I responded,
freely,
thankfully,
spontaneously.
Never mind what I was leaving behind –
my home, friends, livelihood:
the sacrifice seemed more than worth it for the joy of following Jesus.
And one thing's for sure: he didn't disappoint,
his words and deeds being unlike anything I'd seen before,
offering new hope and meaning to life.
I should have been happy with that, of course,
but, like you, I'm human,
and gradually what I'd surrendered began to play on my mind,
niggling within,
especially when Jesus spoke of surrendering yet more –
our very lives –
to serve him.
I wouldn't say it made me doubt or diminished my love for him.
It's simply that I came to understand better
what commitment involves –
what it takes to give and go on giving,
to turn the other cheek,
forgive your enemies,
walk the extra mile –
and that brought home what I hadn't truly grasped:
taking a decision is one thing,
living up to it quite another.
I worried then that I'd be found wanting,
lacking sufficient courage and dedication to see the journey through,
but that's before Jesus hung on the cross,
sacrificing his all.
He asked us to deny ourselves,
to let go of the things of this world,
but he surrendered far more than we ever will
so that we might share life with him.
Never dwell, then, on what you've given up;
celebrate instead what you've received
and what God still holds in store.

Quiet reflection

Prayer

Lord Jesus Christ,
we talk of costly commitment,
of taking up our cross and following you,
but we do not find making *any* sacrifice easy,
let alone the idea of surrendering our all.
Remind us that, whatever you ask of us,
you promise far more,
having opened the way to God's joy, peace and blessing,
not just in this life,
but for all eternity.
Inspire us through your great love,
your selfless acceptance of suffering and death for our sake,
and so help us to offer a little to you,
who gave so much for all.
Amen.

Silence

Comment

We may be called to a distinctive lifestyle, but we are not called to a solitary one, to the life of a hermit or recluse, to a private faith divorced from others. On the contrary, we are to be active in the world, involved with those around us, for faith is something to share, to be lived out in day-to-day life. The gospel is good news, the truth embodied in Jesus setting us free. It is light in our darkness, bringing joy out of sorrow, good out of evil and life out of death. We need to make it known – not through heavy-handed evangelism, beating this or that theological drum, or through seeking to 'convert' people in the way that term is so often understood, but simply through speaking and living in such a way that we communicate something of Jesus to those around us, helping to make more manifest his love, compassion, goodness and mercy to all.

Music *(optional)*

Pilgrims' chorus (Tannhäuser) Wagner

Reading

Mark 1:14-20

Meditation of Andrew

Did I have any doubts, you ask,
any hesitation in following him?
Strangely enough, no.
I should have done, of course,
for I hadn't the slightest idea what I was letting myself in for –
and as for fishing for people,
quite simply, it was Greek to me:
I was none the wiser at all.
Yet somehow that didn't seem to matter.
Nothing did,
except responding to that extraordinary man,
the most amazing person I'd ever met.
It's hard to say what exactly made him so special,
for it was *everything*,
simply the individual he was.
He had this aura about him –
a charisma, you might call it –
that captured your attention and held you spellbound,
or at least it did me.
One look into his eyes told you immediately he was utterly genuine
and altogether unique –
as though he could see into your very soul.
Yet at the same there was welcome there,
acceptance with no strings attached.
So when he called, I followed,
simple as that –
no questions,
no hedging my bets,
just glad and eager response.

What about you?
Would *you* have said yes?
It's an important question,
for he's still calling, you know,
still seeking fishers of people.
The challenge is daunting, I'll give you that,
a journey into the unknown,
but don't dwell on the obstacles.
Look at the man and take the plunge.
You won't regret it.

Quiet reflection

Prayer

Lord Jesus Christ,
help us to respond to your call.
Though we may not be gifted as evangelists,
though we may be awkward and tongue-tied in expressing ourselves,
help us still in some small way,
whether through word or deed,
to witness to you,
our lives speaking of your grace and mercy,
of the hope, joy and peace you so richly give.
Refresh our faith and enliven our commitment,
so that we may be equipped each day to make you known,
testifying through who and what we are to your life-changing power
and redeeming love.
Amen.

Silent retreat

Closing comment

As the old chestnut has it: actions speak louder than words. In terms of being a Christian, that's unquestionably so. Whether we like it or not, people will judge us by what they see in our lives; by what we *say*, certainly, but above all by what we *do*. And if we say one thing yet do another we will open ourselves up to the justifiable charge of hypocrisy. Genuine commitment should express itself in a distinctive lifestyle – in values, attitudes, words and deeds that set us apart. Yes, we'll fail to show those as much as we should. Yes, there will always be aspects of our lives that give out entirely the wrong message. But if we are serious about discipleship we will look to live in such a way that what we say and do are one; to walk, in other words, the way of Christ.

Closing prayer

Lord Jesus Christ,
go with us in our journey of discipleship.
Walk by our side,
correcting when we go astray,
encouraging when we falter,
forgiving when we fail.
Work your miracle of grace within us,
so that we may become more like you,
reflecting something of your love into the darkness of our world.
Help us truly to follow you,
not just with our lips but in our lives,
offered in heartfelt thanks and faithful service.
Amen.

The letter and the spirit

Suggested visual material

Jesus of Nazareth 2 and 3
The Life of Christ II

FIRST SESSION

Introduction

'The law,' Charles Dickens famously wrote in *Oliver Twist*, 'is an ass,' and probably all of us have felt that to be so on many occasions, not least when it's rigidly enforced to the letter in a way that manifestly runs contrary to its intended spirit. Rules may be rules but, dogmatically applied, they can do more harm than good. And that, in a sense, takes us to the heart of Jesus' attitude towards the Law of Moses. Not that he in any way dismissed it; quite the contrary. But he made it clear that when we lose sight of what it's actually all about, what it's designed to achieve, it becomes a hindrance rather than a help. And that's a mistake we can easily make; one, indeed, that has all too often characterised the Church. Unwittingly, we turn faith into doing this, doing that – a matter of outward observance rather than inner devotion. And, as a result, we come to see God as a counsel for the prosecution instead of a loving Father graciously offering forgiveness. Today, we reflect on what Jesus had to say on such matters, and what he continues to say to us.

Opening prayer

Sovereign God,
Lord of heaven and earth, space and time,
we offer you our praise and worship.
Meet with us afresh through our being here today,
for we would know and serve you better.

Open our hearts to the extent of your love,
wonder of your grace
and fullness of your purpose,
so that we may more clearly understand what you have done,
for us and for all,
in Christ.
Help us, as we reflect together,
to celebrate the priceless gift you have given through him:
the truth that sets us free.
Amen.

Comment

Rules are rules, it's often said. We must play things by the book. But, just as a good umpire or referee must sometimes apply discretion when coming to a decision, so too must we in moral issues take each case on its merit rather than resort to blanket judgements. The danger of doing otherwise is graphically illustrated in Jesus' repeated encounters with the Pharisees. Their concern to uphold the letter of the Law blinded them not just to compassion but to common sense. Our next reading reminds us how important it is to look deeper.

Music *(optional)*

Since by man came death (Messiah) Handel

Reading

Mark 2:23–3:6

Meditation of Matthew

They were shocked,
genuinely appalled by what he did and said.
It wasn't a question, in their eyes, of splitting hairs,
dwelling on the fine print –
they really felt he was desecrating the sabbath,
disobeying the Law.

And so he was . . .
technically . . .
yet isn't it sad that anyone can become so fixated on the letter
that they lose sight of the spirit;
so concerned with form
that they abandon sense.
What's it for?
That's the question.
Why did God give us the sabbath in the first place?
And the answer,
surely,
is that it's for *our* benefit,
not *his*.
It doesn't matter to him one iota what we do on it –
whether we work, rest or play –
but it does to *us*,
or at least it should do,
for we each need a break from the routine,
the chance to get away from it all and take our bearings,
remembering there's more to life than the daily grind.
That's what God's concerned about:
our welfare,
our health.
Jesus knew that, even if the Pharisees didn't,
and showed that the sabbath is made for man,
not man for the sabbath.
And it goes further than that:
the Law, prophets, commandments, gospel are for our benefit too –
about what God wants *for* us,
not *from* us.
Don't turn faith into hoops to jump through,
rules to follow,
for that's not just foolish –
it's wrong.
However much you think otherwise,
it won't lead you closer to God,
but will take you further away.

Quiet reflection

Prayer

Loving God,
thank you for setting us free from the Law
with all its demands and duties;
for meeting its requirements in Christ,
paying the price and cancelling the debt.
Save us from subjecting ourselves again to its thrall,
or from creating new burdens to bear in its place;
from turning discipleship into a matter of rules and regulations
that say more about us than they do about you.
Teach us to celebrate the freedom you offer,
the new life opened up through faith,
and help us always to remember that you give not in order to receive
but because you simply delight to bless.
In that knowledge may we joyfully live each day.
Amen.

Silence

Comment

It's easy to condemn the Pharisees for their apparent bigotry and callousness, but we shouldn't be too hasty in pointing the accusing finger. They were, after all, concerned to safeguard the Law that had been given to Moses, and in so doing they were appealing to centuries of tradition, a long line of learned and devout rabbis who had mused upon Scripture and sought to understand its finer points. Daring to challenge that heritage was roughly akin to someone today calling into question our whole legal system, claiming that the various local and national rulings, Acts of Parliament, judges' decisions and the like, that together have fashioned our laws need to be radically overhauled. A degree of scepticism, even hostility, was unsurprising. It takes courage to listen when our preconceptions are challenged. Far easier to close our ears and shut our minds to what we'd rather not consider. Our next reading illustrates the danger of doing precisely that.

Music *(optional)*

God be in my head (Heavenly Light) Geoffrey Nobes

Reading

Mark 7:1-8, 14, 15, 21-23

Meditation of a Pharisee

'You abandon the commandment of God,' he told us,
and hold to human tradition.'
Can you believe the gall of the man!
He actually thinks he understands the Law better than we do –
better than us who've made it our business across the years
to delve into its smallest details,
rummage through the fine print,
ensuring that everything we do,
every last deed,
is in accord with God's wishes,
conforming to his decrees.
And what does Jesus call us for our trouble?
Hypocrites!
It's unbelievable!
He even suggests that the words of Isaiah,
about people worshipping in vain,
somehow apply to *us*;
that we worship with our lips alone
rather than from the heart.
What nonsense!
It was corruption Isaiah censured,
a people who had forgotten the commandments,
transgressed the Law:
the very thing we seek to uphold.
Yet this Jesus thinks he's not just above it,
but its fulfilment –
the one who unfolds its true meaning,
its real intent.

Ah, but he's forgetting one thing:
the Law was *given* to Moses,
not *written* by him.
It was handed down from on high.
So how can Jesus stand there,
condemning human tradition,
when he's flesh and blood like you and I?
It doesn't add up,
surely he sees that.
He's hoist by his own petard,
his teaching, at best, just one interpretation among others,
as human as any,
unless there's something I've overlooked.
I ask you, who does the guy think he is?
God?

Quiet reflection

Prayer

Living God,
teach us what it means truly to honour you,
truly to live as your people.
Help us to understand that you seek not outward show,
nor even obedience to rules and commandments,
but a heart that loves you,
a spirit that seeks you
and a mind that longs to know you better.
Save us from worshipping you with our lips
but being far from you in our lives.
In all we do,
may we be open to your will
and alert to your guidance,
through Jesus Christ our Lord.
Amen.

Silent retreat

SECOND SESSION

Comment

So what was it that Jesus saw as the fulfilment of the Law? What was this commandment that summed up all the others? The answer, of course, is love. And to that statement we'd all nod our heads and murmur theoretical assent, yet when we're faced with complex moral conundrums, the need to make up our minds about this or that controversial issue, love – as a criterion for doing the right thing – can seem woefully vague, to the point that we take refuge once again in reassuring dogma, doctrinaire prescriptions of good and evil, right and wrong. The irony is that though people habitually dismiss talk of love as wishy-washy, an attempt to wriggle off the hook, in reality it is far more demanding than sticking rigidly to the letter of the law, whatever that law may be.

Music *(optional)*

Salut d'Amour Elgar

Reading

John 15:9-17

Meditation of Philip and Thomas

Philip We thought for a minute he was going to give us
a list of rules and regulations.
After all, that's what we were used to,
what we'd grown up with
for as long as we could remember.

Thomas Faith was about doing this, doing that –
not just *ten* commandments,
but a host of others,
decrees for just about every action and eventuality
under the sun.

Philip We're not knocking it,
for it helped to fashion our nation,
and by and large, with the odd aberration,
it's kept us on the straight and narrow.

Thomas But we don't mind admitting that, like many others,
we've found it a struggle,
both to observe the requirements of the Law
and to feel it's got us anywhere,
put us right with God.

Philip Was Jesus going to give us a new system, we wondered,
a different set of rules?

Thomas No, he summed up his way instead in a single sentence,
devastatingly simple,
yet infinitely challenging:

Philip 'This is my commandment:
that you love one another
as I have loved you.'

Thomas Wow, we thought –
that sounds easy!

Philip But, of course, it's not;
in his case it meant death on a cross,
total self-surrender –
that's how costly love can be.

Thomas We'll never show anything quite like that,
but it's the yardstick we measure ourselves by,
the goal we aim for,
shaping everything we think, and say, and do.

Philip It's what the Law, gospel and God himself is all about,
the heart of our faith:
love!

Thomas Not just a new commandment,
but the greatest commandment of all.

Quiet reflection

Prayer

Gracious God,
the good news is so simple and straightforward,
but we make it so complicated,
burying the message of the gospel under a mountain of dogma.
You call us to love you and one another,
just as you love us,
but, instead,
we turn discipleship into jumping through doctrinal hoops,
assenting to theological niceties.
We allow ourselves to be taken in by claims that love is vague,
wishy-washy;
that we need moral absolutes spelt out for each and every situation;
whereas, in fact, love is the most demanding option of all.
Give us the courage, strength and faith we need
to walk the way of Christ.
Amen.

Silence

Comment

Why then appeal to love? Why not impose a uniform standard rather than assess each situation on its merits? The answer is simple: because that's not how God works, his nature being to love and go on loving. It's summed up by one other simple word: grace – his love for the unlovely, the unlovable. We are delivered from the requirements and penalty of the Law through grace alone – forgiven, healed, restored, renewed. Jesus brought a new way of thinking not just about God but about life itself; about what he wants *for* us as well as *from* us.

Music *(optional)*

Amazing Grace Traditional hymn

Reading

John 1:1-18

Meditation of the Apostle John

What's it all about, they ask me?
What does Jesus bring that we didn't have before?
Well, I've thought about that over the years,
pondered what it is that makes him so special,
and if I had to sum it up in one word,
it would be this:
grace!
That's what sets him apart from others,
what makes the difference between the old and the new.
Moses brought us the Law,
precious undoubtedly,
serving us well for centuries,
but it put the onus on us to live up to it –
to observe its decrees and perform its rituals,
following its prescriptions as best we could.
The way of Christ is so very different,
for it speaks of a new covenant
written not on tablets of stone but in our hearts –
a relationship with God based on what he has done
rather than anything we might do.
Yes, we fall short of what he wants us to be.
Yes, we fail him time and again.
Yes, we are unworthy of his love and undeserving of mercy.
But none of that matters,
for God has made the running,
accomplished what we could never achieve on our own.
Don't settle for less.
Don't struggle against the odds to put yourself right with him,
striving somehow to earn his blessing.
Reach out and accept what he longs to give.
From his fullness we have all received . . .
grace upon grace.

Quiet reflection

Prayer

Loving God,
we know we fall short,
that we repeatedly fail you,
that we have no right to your love or claim on your mercy,
and such knowledge hangs heavy upon us,
filling us with frustration and remorse.
Yet we know also that you are slow to anger and swift to forgive,
your desire being to pardon rather than punish,
to redeem, renew and restore.
For your grace revealed in Christ
and the fresh start you daily make possible through him,
receive our praise.
Amen.

Silent retreat

Closing comment

Too often the Church has come across as judgemental, self-righteously pronouncing on matters of right and wrong, truth and falsehood, and woe betide any who disagree. We too, through adhering to an inflexible moral code, can sometimes set ourselves up as judge and jury, adopting a holier-than-thou attitude that looks down condescendingly on all who see things differently from how we do. And the tragedy is we can convince ourselves that in so doing we're honouring God, upholding a proper understanding of what he requires. Before we cast the first stone we need to remind ourselves of what Jesus had to say on the subject, and the way, time and again, he overturned people's expectations, seemingly flying in the face of everything the Law required. The way of love may sometimes be dismissed as easy, but that couldn't be more wrong, for, properly understood, it's more demanding than any other: simple yet radical, costly yet infinitely rewarding. And if we're serious about following Jesus it's not just one way among others; it's the *only* way.

Closing prayer

Lord Jesus Christ,
thank you for meeting through your death the requirements of the Law
and liberating us from its demands;
for setting us free from all that would hold us captive.
Forgive us for sometimes losing sight of that –
for making your love conditional on doing or saying the right things
instead of gladly responding from the heart.
Help us to understand that the Law and the prophets,
everything you require,
is summed up in that one simple yet challenging command:
to love –
and in loving others may we more truly love you.
Amen.

Look and learn

Suggested visual material

Jesus of Nazareth 2–4
The Life of Christ II

FIRST SESSION

Introduction

All of us, no doubt, hope to grow in faith, but when did you last actively seek to do that? How long has it been, for example, since you read the Bible truly searching for fresh insight? When did you last seriously wrestle with aspects of faith you find hard to understand? It's often said we don't get something for nothing, and that's as true when it comes to maturing in faith as anywhere. If we seriously want to learn more, we must be ready to search and keep on searching; earnestly and doggedly to seek before we find. Only then can we expect to move forward in discipleship. Today, through readings, silence and reflection, we explore the challenge but also the promise that brings.

Opening prayer

Great and wonderful God,
we want to learn more of you,
to grow in faith and understanding
and grasp more fully what you have done for us in Christ.
We want to recognise the immensity of your love,
breadth of your mercy
and scope of your power;
to celebrate the glorious possibilities –
now and for all eternity –
you have opened up for us through him.

Help us now,
as we take time out from the daily routine of life,
to hear your voice afresh
and to discover more of what it means to know and love you.
Amen.

Comment

From almost the very start of his ministry, Jesus was pursued by crowds intent on seeking him out. Why did they do so? The answers are many. Some were drawn by the signs and wonders he performed. Some were captivated by his words. Some were intrigued by his growing reputation. And some, no doubt, were fascinated by the controversy that invariably seemed to surround him. Motives, in other words, were mixed, yet that didn't matter. The important thing was that their curiosity was aroused, that they wanted to know more about Jesus: who he was and what he had to offer. Can the same be said of us?

Music *(optional)*

Seek and you will find (Across the Water) Keith Duke

Reading

Mark 1:29-39

Meditation of Simon Peter

It wasn't just *us* searching for him;
it was *everyone*,
or so it seemed at the time –
a never-ending procession coming up with the same question:
where's he gone?
And the truth is we'd no more idea than any of them,
for Jesus had got up during the night
and vanished.

We found him later,
out on the hills, deep in contemplation,
and we assumed he'd simply gone to spend time with God,
to pray and reflect on his calling.
Looking back, though, I wonder if there was more to it than that:
whether there was a lesson behind his disappearance,
as important for you and me as for any.
You see, he knew the crowds would be clamouring after him,
his name being the talk of the town after the wonders he'd performed,
so why not milk the applause,
make the most of a receptive audience while he could?
That's what *I'd* have done in his place.
But not Jesus:
quite the opposite.
He wanted them to *look* for him,
to seek until they found,
and by that he meant finding not just *him*
but the truth of who he was,
the meaning of his message,
the reason he'd come.
That's what he was after:
not admirers or thrill-seekers drawn by his signs and wonders,
but people hungry to know more
and truly ready to search.
They'd glimpsed a little
but there was more to discover,
more to be revealed –
and the same is true for us.
Seek,
and you *will* find.

Quiet reflection

Prayer

Saviour Christ,
what do we look for in you?
We like to think that it's truth, light and life,

but in reality our motives are less exalted:
more about the secular than the sacred,
about *our ends* rather than *your will*.
Teach us to long to know you better,
to seek your way
and to yearn for deeper faith and understanding,
so that in searching we may truly find.
Amen.

Silence

Comment

We've spoken already of the mixed motives people had for seeking out Jesus, and one such is apparent in our next reading. A woman from Syrophoenicia approached Jesus for one reason only: to have her daughter made well. Nothing else was of any concern to her; the only thing that mattered was the health of her loved one. In her cry of desperation we will recognise a common human trait: that of turning to Jesus in times of need. So often we put faith to one side until crisis strikes, to the point that for the rest of the time it's almost incidental to our lives. It's only when circumstances veer unexpectedly out of control that we're suddenly eager to know Jesus better, to re-establish contact. Selfish and superficial that may be, but he does not condemn us for it. On the contrary, he welcomes our desire to seek his help. Never feel you have no right to do so, however much you may have forgotten him in the past. If *he* thinks otherwise, who are we to argue?

Music *(optional)*

De profundis (Across the Water) Keith Duke

Reading

Mark 7:24-37

Meditation of the Syrophoenician woman

He was exhausted, poor man,
emotionally and physically drained,
and I felt guilty about troubling him,
adding still more to the weight on his shoulders.
Yet I was desperate, you'll understand that,
for my daughter was dreadfully disturbed,
and I feared not only for her sanity
but also for her life.
We needed help,
urgently,
every avenue we'd tried having proved fruitless –
a blind alley,
false dawn.
So, despite being a woman and a Gentile,
expected to keep my distance,
I knocked on the door of that house,
and waited.
He'd really hoped to escape notice,
can you believe that?
Despite the wonders he'd performed –
the healing he'd brought,
joy given,
faith restored,
love shown –
he still dared to believe he could melt into the shadows,
away from it all.
Was he simply tired?
Or was he troubled by the celebrity status,
by the crowds coming to gawp and marvel?
I don't know,
but I knew this:
he, if anyone, could answer my prayer.
And he did!
When he saw my need,
he responded,
testing my motives, it's true,
but unable finally to turn his back and look the other way.

Unlike others,
and more than anyone else I've ever met,
he really cared,
enough to give and go on giving.
He was all in,
fit to drop,
urgently needing time for himself.
But though that mattered to him,
thankfully,
wonderfully,
I mattered more.

Quiet reflection

Prayer

Loving God,
remind us that,
whoever we are,
whatever we have done,
you care for us,
each of us being special,
precious in your sight.
Teach us that if we truly seek you,
we *will* find,
that if we lay before you our needs,
you *will* respond,
not necessarily in the way we expect,
but nonetheless answering our prayer.
Give us faith in your purpose
and trust in your power,
assured that, though sometimes we have far too little time for *you*,
always you have time for *us*.
Amen.

Silent retreat

SECOND SESSION

Comment

Mixed motives for seeking him may be acceptable to Jesus, but they can be hugely destructive nonetheless. They can close our lives to real and meaningful discovery, causing us never to look any deeper, a case in point being recorded in our next reading. Crowds thronged round Jesus with one thing in mind: they had no food and wanted him to feed them. He was more than happy to do so, his concern embracing their physical as well as spiritual needs, but he wanted to meet those underlying needs too; to offer them life in all its fullness. He wants the same for us. Faith can become just another accessory, understood as a way of securing God's blessing and approval of our comfortable lifestyles. Instead of stretching us it seals us in a vacuum, precluding fresh insights and experiences. Let that happen, and though Jesus longs to open our eyes to so much more, we will never find it.

Music *(optional)*

Adagio un poco mosso (Piano Concerto No. 5) Beethoven

Reading

John 6:24-35

Meditation of Andrew

It's true what he said:
they pursued him, not so much because of his message –
because they were hungry to learn of God –
but because they'd been *physically* hungry
and he'd given them something to eat.
Their thoughts were of earth,
not heaven;
of what he could do for them in the here and now,
not in the life to come.

Never mind their immortal souls –
it was their bodies that concerned them,
whether they were clothed, housed, fed and watered,
with money in their pockets and food on the table.
He offered so much –
eternal life –
and they failed to see it,
each so concerned with the rewards of this world
that they'd eyes for nothing else.
Oh yes, they played the part of devoted followers to a tee,
pursuing him everywhere,
walking in his footsteps,
but they didn't really follow,
not as he'd hoped.
They were hangers-on,
out for what they could get,
intent finally on serving self rather than him.
and the irony is that though he gave his all,
they failed to receive.
Don't make that mistake.
Don't accept crusts when you can have bread of life,
food for your soul.
He offers eternal nourishment –
don't settle for less.

Quiet reflection

Prayer

Eternal God,
you offer us so much in Christ –
joy,
hope,
peace,
forgiveness,
assurance,
wholeness,

love –
but while we pay lip service to such blessings,
so often we fail to make them our own.
Day after day we forget you,
barely giving you a moment's thought,
only remembering you in time of need.
But then we expect you to respond –
to deliver us from a crisis,
redeem a situation,
provide the answers we seek.
Teach us that you want to give us so much more –
life in all its fullness, lived with you –
and help us to receive that,
with glad thanksgiving.
Amen.

Silence

Comment

It's tempting to think that we would never make the same mistake as those who followed Jesus simply because they were hungry or in need of help. Our faith, we tell ourselves, is deeper, wiser. We've grasped the truth and understood just what he has to offer. And we're eager to learn more, to seek out further insights. No danger of us closing our minds. Yet we couldn't be more wrong, for religious people as much as any – perhaps *more* than any – can do precisely that. We can assume that we've learnt the ropes, grasped the essentials, and all that remains is to fill in the occasional gap. A mature faith, by contrast, is open to being stretched, challenged and revised. It is always in the making, never the finished article. Forget that, and our convictions can be more of a hindrance than a help.

Music *(optional)*

The light of God (Heavenly Light) Geoffrey Nobes

Reading

John 5:36b-47

Meditation of John the Evangelist

He was right, you know,
about them searching the Scriptures,
no one doing that more diligently than the scribes.
It was their life's work,
what set them apart,
almost every waking hour, it seemed, spent reading,
studying,
dissecting,
debating,
so that they knew the last jot and tittle of the Law,
the exact words of the prophets,
every detail of God's holy word, inside out and back to front.
They, if anyone, should have recognised Jesus for who he was,
for so much in Scripture pointed to him:
'A child has been born to us,
a son given.'
'From you, Bethlehem, one of the little towns of Judah,
will emerge a ruler of Israel,
whose roots go back to earliest times.'
'Nations will be drawn to your light,
and kings to the brightness of your dawn.'
'The spirit of the Lord will rest upon him,
of wisdom and understanding,
counsel and might,
knowledge and fear of the Lord' –
all this, and so much more, fulfilled in him,
the bringer of life,
Word made flesh,
but they could not see for looking.
He was the one they sought,
yet could not find;
the one they longed for,
yet turned away,

not only rejecting him,
but nailing him to a cross.
And even there the truth was plain,
the Scriptures again fulfilled:
'He was oppressed and afflicted,
yet his mouth remained closed.'
'He was wounded for our iniquities,
broken for our sins;
his was the punishment that made us whole,
and by his bruises we are healed.'
They searched,
yet sought in vain,
for, important though it is,
it's not finally in Scripture that the answer lies,
but in the man.
I wonder, can they see it now?

Quiet reflection

Prayer

Living God,
thank you for the Bible
and for the way you speak to us through it.
Thank you for the way that, through its pages,
we can trace your activity across history,
your dealings with your people,
your call, guidance, will and mercy.
Teach us to read and study the Scriptures thoughtfully,
eagerly,
carefully,
prayerfully,
seeking within them your guidance for our daily lives,
but save us from elevating them into your place,
from ascribing to them an authority that is yours and yours alone.
Grant that our faith may rest finally, not on the written word,
but on the Word made flesh,

Jesus Christ our Lord,
through whom you have supremely spoken and continue to speak,
and in whose name we pray.
Amen.

Silent retreat

Closing comment

All of us, no doubt, started off our journey of Christian discipleship enthusiastically seeking to know more. We probably pored over our Bibles, eagerly read devotional material, prayed at every opportunity, and sought out other Christians with whom to talk about matters of faith. But typically that first flush of enthusiasm fades over the years. We become careless, even blasé about it, no longer making the time for God we once did. We no longer expect to grow, no longer even see the need to do so. Talk of knowing Christ can become just that: talk. And our faith gets stuck in a rut as a result. Do you still seek, as you once did, to know him better? Do you still search for understanding? And, if not, is it time you did something about it?

Closing prayer

Lord Jesus Christ,
though we talk of growing in faith,
of seeking and finding,
we fail to look for new insights as often
or as eagerly
as we should.
We grow careless,
lazy,
complacent,
assuming we have grasped all there is to know
and that we have no need to stretch our horizons further.
Forgive us,
and teach us to hunger and thirst after righteousness,
assured that, if we truly search,

we shall be filled.
Send us out with a burning desire to learn more of you,
and may that flame never be extinguished.
Amen.

Can it be true?

Suggested visual material

Jesus of Nazareth 3 and 4
The Life of Christ II

FIRST SESSION

Introduction

Few, if any of us, will never have questioned certain aspects of Christian belief. It would be surprising if we didn't, for the gospel concerns realities beyond this world, truths that stretch and often defy comprehension. There's nothing wrong with admitting we can't get our heads round such things; indeed, only by doing so can we hope to find the answers we're looking for. Today, through reflecting on questions put to Jesus during the course of his ministry, we're going to explore some of the issues we may wrestle with in turn, and how best we might approach our own questions of faith.

Opening prayer

Mighty and mysterious God,
greater than our highest thoughts,
above and beyond words or human fathoming,
in awe and wonder we worship you.
We praise you for making yourself known in Christ,
revealing your love to us in a way we can relate to.
Yet we know that our knowledge of you will,
at best,
always be partial,
much defying our comprehension.
Give us the faith we need to live with questions
and to face them honestly,

so that they may lead us into deeper truth:
a fuller recognition of who and what you are
and of your loving purpose for all.
Amen.

Comment

Believing in God isn't easy, for – as we've said – it takes us into the realms of that which defies human language and stretches our minds to the limit. We cannot hear or see God in the way we hear and see other things. We cannot prove his existence or even adequately define him. We struggle to reconcile what we believe with numerous aspects of daily life. All of that can make Christian belief seem far removed from the real world, to the point that we dismiss it altogether. Yet if we find it hard sometimes to keep faith, we should remember that many have struggled likewise before us. So it was for Nicodemus, whom we'll hear about in a moment in our first reading. A respected and learned rabbi, he of all people might have been expected to have no problem discussing the finer points of religion, yet when he came to Jesus seeking greater enlightenment he was to find himself hopelessly out of his depth, his mind reeling as he tried to take in what Jesus was telling him. He wanted answers to his questions, loose ends tied up, but instead had to take things on trust. Do we have sufficient wisdom and humility to do the same?

Music *(optional)*

The mirror of the Trinity (Magnificat) Praetorius

Reading

John 3:1-17

Meditation of Nicodemus

I didn't know if I was coming or going.
One moment he was talking about himself,
the next, of God,

and the next, of the Spirit,
almost as though they were same thing.
I'd seen already that God was working through him,
even if my fellow Pharisees struggled with the idea –
how else could you explain what he was doing?
But as we talked together he seemed to imply more than that:
that he spoke for the Father himself,
and somehow, in his own person, brought the Spirit among us.
I was baffled,
mystified,
yet he didn't seem surprised –
if anything, the opposite.
Oh, he teased me a little,
pointing out that, as a teacher of Israel,
I, of all people, should have known such things,
but, if I understand him correctly,
he didn't so much expect me to unravel the mystery
as to accept that I can't;
to realise that it *is* a mystery,
and always will be.
God as three persons –
could he seriously be suggesting that?
It's preposterous, surely,
even blasphemy,
yet somehow I've not been able to dismiss it from my mind,
for in a strange way it seems to make sense.
He *did* show me God, as no other has done,
and the Spirit moved not only through *him*,
but also through those followers of his,
almost as though he'd passed it on
and was still with them after he'd died.
It's hard to believe,
impossible to believe:
that God is three in one yet one in three.
Yet do you know what?
I really think it's true!

Quiet reflection

Prayer

Almighty God,
teach us to live with the mystery of who you are,
to recognise that though we can never fully articulate,
let alone understand,
the wonder of your being,
we can experience it nonetheless,
responding to you each day as Father, Son and Holy Spirit.
However much it defies logic
and stretches imagination to the limit,
may we know and honour you as God above us,
God beside us,
God within us,
three in one yet one in three.
Help us to worship you in all your splendour,
glimpsing in your varied faces the Lord of all,
your glory filling the universe
yet touching our lives,
your purpose transcending space and time
yet enfolding us in eternity.
Almighty God,
different yet ever the same,
we praise you.
Amen.

Silence

Comment

Some statements of belief are hard to accept, for two reasons. First, they are impossible to prove, seeming to fly in the face of everything we see and know about the world. Second, they can appear too good to be true, little more than wishful thinking, hopeless naïveté. Nowhere is that more so than with the Christian belief in resurrection, the promise of life beyond death. We want to believe it, we try to believe it and, yes, we *do* believe it, but always we have questions in the back of our minds. How can it be? How is it possible for life to continue after we've breathed our last and this body of ours has turned to dust? Does our faith have firm foundations or are we merely deluding ourselves? Like Jairus in our next reading, we automatically see death as the end, and struggle to look beyond it. Yet the message of the gospel revolves around the empty tomb and risen Lord, the one who lived and continues to live among us. 'The sure and certain hope of the resurrection to eternal life' – can it be true? The experience and testimony of generations across the years is a resounding Yes!

Music *(optional)*

Pié Jesu (Reqiuem) Andrew Lloyd Webber

Reading

Mark 5:21-43

Meditation of Jairus

They were thinking not just of *him*,
but of me too,
wanting to spare me getting my hopes up
only to have them dashed.
I'd set off that day hoping against hope,
believing that if anyone could help my daughter
it was Jesus –
the talk of the town.
So imagine my joy when he agreed to come with me,
my frustration when he was distracted
by that woman reaching out to touch his cloak,
and then my despair when news came through
that my daughter had died.
It was too late for help,
too late for anything –
there was nothing more that anyone could do.
At least that's what we assumed,
until Jesus carried on regardless,

striding into the house,
shooing away the mourners,
and calmly commanding, 'Little girl, get up!'
And the astonishing thing is, she *did*,
can you believe it!
Quick as a flash she was up and about,
as if nothing had happened,
right as rain.
He'd defeated death itself,
my daughter brought back to life,
and we were overcome with gratitude, relief and delight.
They tell me he promises the same for us all:
that we too can rise again.
Can it be so?
Can the last enemy truly be conquered,
its power destroyed?
I don't know how even Jesus could do that,
but I don't need to know,
for I saw my daughter raised,
and that's good enough for me.
'Do not fear,' he said,
'only believe,'
and, despite my doubts,
my many unanswered questions,
Lord, I *do*.

Quiet reflection

Prayer

Gracious God,
you tell us not to fear but to believe,
to trust that, whatever we're called to face,
in life or in death,
you are able to see us through.
We *try* to believe,
truly want to,

but we struggle at times,
for so much in the world seems to challenge our faith,
denying your loving purpose.
We know that not every problem is resolved as we would wish,
that healing is not always granted,
that catastrophe can strike at any time
and that death comes finally to us all,
and such knowledge casts a shadow over our hopes,
leaving us afraid and uncertain.
Teach us that though commitment to you
brings no immunity from life's ills,
no guarantee of a trouble-free path,
you will be there to help, come what may,
ready to strengthen, comfort, support and sustain.
Help us truly to believe in your transforming power,
now and always.
Amen.

Silent retreat

SECOND SESSION

Comment

Pick up a newspaper or listen to the daily news and, if you are a thinking person, you will soon find your faith challenged. A natural disaster claiming the lives of hundreds, innocent children dying of disease or starvation, injustice blighting the lives of communities, evil seeming to prosper while good goes unrewarded – how do we make sense of God in relation to such things? How can we continue to talk of his love, mercy and goodness when, for so many people, those are conspicuous by their absence? At the very least, we are forced to reflect on what we believe and to wrestle with the inconsistency between the way things are and the way we believe they should be. Yet the fact that we don't have all the answers doesn't mean we should throw out the baby with the bathwater. Some truths will always be beyond us, needing to be taken on trust. Though we cannot always see it, in the apparent arbitrariness of life, with all its suffering and sorrow, God is nonetheless there, somehow working out his loving purpose despite all that militates against it.

Music *(optional)*

Hear the cry (The New Dawn) Margaret Rizza

Reading

Mark 13:1-8

Meditation of James

Things can only get better:
that's what some will tell you,
either because they hope it,
life being hard,
or because they expect it,
convinced the world must automatically improve.
But I'm telling you this,
don't take it for granted,
for in this life it simply isn't true.
Oh, things *can* get better, don't get me wrong.
I'm not some doom merchant
suggesting we might as well give up now.
Quite the contrary:
there's much to anticipate,
every reason to look forward,
for in all kinds of ways,
large and small,
the kingdom is growing among us,
Yet that doesn't mean its coming is imminent,
for sometimes things have to get worse before they can improve –
the boil lanced, if you like,
the wound cleaned,
before the patient can heal.

The world's not perfect
and neither are we –
so much still denying what God wants us to be,
but though much frustrates his purpose,
still he continues to work,
seeking to turn all things to good.
So don't be dismayed by disaster –
by trials that come upon you –
for they not only *will* happen, but *must*,
refining like fire until all is made new.
Whatever testing you face,
keep faith,
hold firm,
and trust in the future God holds in store,
for, by his grace and in the fullness of time,
things not only *can* get better;
they most certainly *will*!

Quiet reflection

Prayer

Mighty God,
it's hard to keep faith sometimes,
hard to believe in your power and love
in the face of the suffering that besets so many,
the tragedies that scar our world,
the pain, hatred and violence
that you seemingly allow to go unchecked.
We are left shaken by it all,
mystified,
our faith on occasions hanging by a thread,
for how can anyone,
let alone you,
permit such evils to continue?
Help us to live with questions,
trusting that, despite what seems to deny your purpose,
you are nonetheless at work.

Teach us that though in this world much conspires against you,
the time is coming when your will shall be done
and your kingdom come –
a time when there will be no more tears,
no more darkness,
no more death,
but all will dwell in the light of your love,
for ever.
Amen.

Silence

Comment

Most of our questions arise from what we struggle to understand. But not all. Some, as our next reading reminds us, stem from something very different: from what we'd rather *not* understand, what we don't want to accept, what we'd rather ignore. It may be that believing something asks more of us than we're willing to give, or that it clashes with our view of the world, or that it simply unsettles us. Whatever the case, the result can be that we turn our backs on it, preferring to reject the idea out of hand rather than face up to its challenge. Allow that to happen and, far from deepening faith, our questions will undermine it completely.

Music *(optional)*

Credo (Mass in B minor) J. S. Bach

Reading

John 6:56-69

Meditation of Simon Peter

They were abandoning him en masse,
no longer interested in following,
and I could sympathise to a point,
for his teaching was hard,
confusing,
difficult to comprehend.
We were all at sea ourselves,
me included,
the idea of Jesus giving his body and blood for the life of the world
seeming bizarre,
brutal,
even barbaric.
Yet just because we couldn't make sense of it
didn't make it untrue –
it showed rather how much we'd still to learn.
That's what so many forgot.
They set themselves up as judge and jury,
deciding that they knew best;
that whatever challenged their view of the world
must necessarily be false.
We're all guilty of that sometimes, of course,
but it can't be right,
for how else can we be opened to new horizons,
enabled to learn and grow?
Yes, we were perplexed, like I said,
disturbed by what he taught,
but we'd followed Jesus thus far,
and heard enough,
seen enough,
experienced enough in that time
to understand that he spoke not only *of* God
but *for* God,
bringing heaven down to earth,
the divine here among us.
We've much yet to grasp,
a long way to go,
but we're determined to continue,

to walk with Jesus as best we can,
for in him we've glimpsed the truth,
words of eternal life.
To whom else should we go for that?

Quiet reflection

Prayer

Lord Jesus Christ,
we don't know you as fully as we should,
we don't understand as much about you as we would like,
and we don't always find following you as easy as we hope.
There is much that puzzles us,
that challenges and even undermines our faith,
and there are times when we feel like giving up,
our commitment sorely tested.
Yet in you we have glimpsed the face of God,
grace and truth unlike anything this world can offer,
and we cannot let go,
for where else could we turn to find the life you promise?
Help us, despite our doubts and questions,
to keep faith with you.
Weak and foolish though we may be,
help us to walk your way.
Amen.

Silent retreat

Closing comment

The person who has never doubted has in all probability never truly believed, for really to accept something means to make it one's own, facing up to and working through the challenges it presents. Questions are an integral part of faith, a sign indeed of its health, provided that we do not expect to find easy answers and lose heart should we fail to do so. That's the acid test: how we respond when questions arise. Too easily we move from doubt to disbelief, especially when keeping faith means opening our lives to what we'd rather not face. Yet when we're ready to wrestle honestly with what troubles or confuses, to seek for understanding and to go on searching, our questions can lead us to deeper insights, greater understanding. Have we the humility, trust and commitment necessary to enable that to happen?

Closing prayer

Lord Jesus Christ,
there is much we don't understand,
much that leaves us puzzled and even troubled.
Yet in you we have found light and life,
peace unlike anything this world can give,
an answer to our innermost needs.
In that knowledge may we see our questions
not as obstacles but as opportunities,
opening the way to new horizons and fresh discoveries –
to a stronger and deeper faith.
Amen.

The bigger picture

Suggested visual material

Jesus of Nazareth 4 and 6
The Life of Christ IV

FIRST SESSION

Introduction

'Your God is too small,' wrote the celebrated theologian J. B. Phillips in his 1961 book of the same title, and that message can probably be applied to each one of us. Another way of wording it would be this: your Christ is too small – for the two are one and the same. However profound our conception of Jesus, however wonderful we consider him to be, he is greater still, able to do far more than we can ever ask or even think of. Today, through readings and reflection, we consider how his followers during his earthly ministry found their horizons stretched, their vision broadened. Their experiences remind us that we, like them, need always to be open to the bigger picture, if we would truly know God.

Opening prayer

God of all,
open our minds to your greatness,
your awesome power and love.
Open our hearts to your grace and mercy.
Open our souls to your healing touch,
your transforming and redeeming purpose.
Open our lives to everything you have done,
are doing,
and will continue to do
through Jesus Christ our Lord.

In him,
with him
and through him,
may we live and move and have our being.
Amen.

Comment

Taking things literally isn't always a good idea, for sometimes words point beyond themselves to a deeper truth. We use similes, metaphor, analogy and so forth to stretch their meaning, opening up new horizons, fresh possibilities for understanding. Get hung up on what language strictly seems to say and we may miss what it's actually all about, just as many did in the incident recorded in our next reading. So tied were they to a literal interpretation of Jesus' words that their minds were closed to the bigger picture. It's a mistake we can all too easily make.

Music *(optional)*

Credo in unum Deum (Mass in C minor) Mozart

Reading

John 6:35, 41-51

Meditation of one of the crowd listening to Jesus

What's he on about?
Has the guy taken leave of his senses?
He's an ordinary person, like you and me,
living, breathing, flesh and blood,
so what's all this poppycock about coming down from heaven?
And as for being living bread,
that's not just daft but close to blasphemy,
for its plain what he's alluding to –
how, centuries ago, God sent down manna from heaven –
nourishment in the wilderness,
sustenance in time of need.

You've spotted what he's suggesting, surely:
that our lives are somehow a desert,
and only he can help us through.
Well I'm sorry, but we know different.
He's Joseph's son,
not God's.
We know his family,
his home,
his past,
his present.
And unless the divine can also be human,
the word become flesh,
he simply hasn't a leg to stand on.
It's a shame, really,
for he's a decent chap –
means well,
talks a lot of sense
and has truly done good –
but when he harps on about all that spiritual stuff,
talking of true bread,
his body,
the gift of life,
I just can't see where he's coming from.
Am I missing something?

Quiet reflection

Prayer

Sovereign God,
thank you that you are not remote from us,
detached in splendid isolation,
but that, having shared our humanity in Christ,
you are with us now,
each moment of every day,
through your Spirit.

Thank you that we can know and see you
not only in prayer and worship,
but also in the fellowship of your people,
the world around us
and the circumstances and events of daily life.
Teach us, always, to look beneath the surface,
beyond what we think we know and understand,
and to glimpse your presence in the ordinary and familiar.
Remind us that, through Jesus, heaven has touched earth,
the divine been made human,
the gulf between us been overcome.
Amen.

Silence

Comment

When the disciples first responded to the call of Jesus, they had little idea who he really was. They followed simply because they recognised in him something different, special – a man who spoke and acted with an authority unlike anything they'd seen before. But it was only gradually that they grasped he came from God, that he made God known, that he was – in some way they couldn't quite pin down – God himself. Bit by bit the truth dawned on them that he came not to rule but to serve, to establish a kingdom not on earth but in heaven, to bring life to the world by surrendering his own. In our next reading, we see how Peter, James and John moved one step closer to grasping that bigger picture.

Music *(optional)*

Gloria (Mass in B minor) J. S. Bach

Reading

Mark 9:2-9

Meditation of the Apostle John

What happened that day up on the mountain?
I'm still not sure, even now.
Maybe it was the altitude addling the brain
or perhaps the light playing tricks,
but one moment we seemed to be looking at Jesus –
and the next it was as though he were God himself,
his face radiant,
his clothes dazzling white,
his whole being bathed in light, too bright to behold.
And that's not all,
for there beside him stood Moses and Elijah,
epitomising the Law and prophets,
as though everything that had gone before –
our life, our faith, our history –
had been leading up to that moment,
finding fulfilment in this man standing before us.
We didn't grasp all that at first, of course;
in fact we didn't grasp much –
just stood there gawping,
awestruck,
until I blurted out some nonsense about building shelters for them all –
but we realised afterwards we'd been granted a glimpse of glory,
a sign that this man whom we loved and followed
was more special than we'd begun to imagine,
too special for words.
We wanted to stay there for ever,
to keep hold of that mountaintop experience,
but life's not like that, sadly.
Like faith, it must be lived out in the daily routine,
in this world of ups and downs,
highs and lows,
and, believe me, we were to have both of those aplenty.
But whatever the trials we were to face –
the depths of despair, suffering and human evil –
there was no way those could have the final word.
We'd seen the light that day –
literally –
and it would never be extinguished.

Quiet reflection

Prayer

Lord Jesus Christ,
we think we have grasped the wonder of who and what you are . . .
but we haven't.
We think we understand the extent of your love . . .
but we don't.
We think we can fathom the breadth of your power and goodness . . .
but we can't.
Teach us that there is always more to be revealed of your truth,
more to learn of your mercy,
and more to discover of your purpose,
your glory being far beyond anything we can fully comprehend.
Give us a greater sense of your greatness,
a fuller awareness of all you have done, are doing and continue to do,
and keep us open each day to fresh insights,
new horizons
and deeper experiences of your unsurpassable grace.
Amen.

Silent retreat

SECOND SESSION

Comment

Don't run before you can walk, we sometimes say. In other words, take things step by step, mastering one skill before progressing to another. That's true of all aspects of learning. There's no point, for example, in grappling with the niceties of trigonometry if we haven't first grasped basic mathematical principles. It's futile, similarly, trying to translate another language without first acquainting ourselves, at least in part, with its grammar and vocabulary. We must understand the fundamentals before we're ready to advance further. That's a lesson the apostles repeatedly had to learn about faith, even after they'd been following Jesus for three years, hanging on to his every word and witnessing firsthand his countless signs and wonders. You might have thought, by then, they'd have fully understood who he was and what he came to do, but in fact their knowledge was partial to say the least. They'd come a long way – literally and spiritually – but they still had further to go, and there could be no shortcuts. For all they had learnt, much remained beyond them, and would only become clear when they were ready for it. So it is for us all.

Music *(optional)*

Send forth your Spirit (Fountain of Life) Margaret Rizza

Reading

John 15:26, 27; 16:4b-15

Meditation of Peter, James and John

Peter There were things he felt unable to tell us at the time,
not because he didn't want to or had something to hide,
but because we simply weren't ready to hear them.
John We weren't expecting his death, for a start,
each of us still secretly hoping he'd reign on earth,
here and now.
James And if we weren't prepared for his death,
we weren't ready either for his resurrection.
None of us believed the tomb was empty,
not at first.
We thought it was nonsense, do you recall?
John It was his return to the Father, though, that got me most –
I just couldn't get my head round it.
One moment he was back by our side,
and the next gone again,
or so it seemed at the time.

Peter And as for the gift of Spirit,
power from on high,
well, he may have promised it often enough,
but we'd no idea what he actually meant.
It took us by surprise completely!
John Yes, we've come a long way
since we rode with him into Jerusalem,
the crowds welcoming him as king.
He'd told us what to expect,
but we couldn't even take *that* in at first,
let alone more.
James And he continues to astonish us, even now,
the Spirit, time and again,
offering fresh insights into the things he taught us.
Peter We needed time to learn,
to accept,
to grow,
and, of course, we still do,
for we're talking here of the things of God,
of grasping the unseen.
James It needs patience to do that,
John trust,
Peter discipline,
James a life lived with him.
John We're on a journey of faith,
James and we've not finished it yet,
Peter not by a long way.
All We've only just begun.

Quiet reflection

Prayer

Mighty and mysterious God,
we like to think we know it all –
that we have understood the gospel
and grasped the wonder of who and what you are.

But the reality is different,
for your ways are not our ways
or your thoughts our thoughts.
So much is beyond us,
leaving us baffled and bemused,
and much else is at best only partially fathomed.
Time and again what we thought we knew is challenged and tested,
needing to be either revised or discarded altogether.
Give us the humility we need
to accept that our knowledge is incomplete,
that there is always more to learn.
Open our hearts to the great adventure of discovery you set before us,
until that day when we finally see you face to face,
and know you, even as we are fully known.
Amen.

Silence

Comment

For the followers of Jesus, his death seemed a catastrophe, the end of everything they'd hoped for and believed. They'd been convinced that Jesus was the Messiah, but clearly they'd been wrong, for how could God's promised deliverer end up nailed to a cross? It didn't make sense. Such questions, of course, were to be wonderfully answered as Jesus appeared among them, risen and victorious. They realised then that he was indeed the one they'd waited for, only far greater and more special than they'd begun to imagine. Whereas previously they'd been broken at the thought of him being taken from them, now when he spoke of leaving them to return to the Father they took the news quite calmly, confident that, through his Spirit, he would nonetheless always be with them. Their understanding of Jesus – who he was and what he had accomplished – had not only grown, but would continue to grow: an ever-expanding picture.

Music *(optional)*

Worthy is the lamb that was slain (Messiah) Handel

Reading

Luke 14:44-53

Meditation of Philip

You'd think we'd have been dismayed, wouldn't you –
to lose Jesus again, so soon after he'd come back to us?
After all, we'd been shattered the first time,
left floundering like fish out of water once deprived of his presence.
True, this time was different –
no cross,
no agony, torment and death –
but he was gone nonetheless,
snatched away from us once more.
Only he *wasn't*,
that's the strange thing.
He was with us much more meaningfully,
not in the flesh but in Spirit –
around us,
beside us,
beyond us,
within us,
touching our lives in every part.
I can't quite explain it,
but suddenly we knew he was closer than we'd ever dreamt –
for he was not just the Messiah,
the risen Lord,
but God himself,
one with him,
one with us,
the divine in human form.
We'd walked and talked with him,
and we finally realised that we'd do so always, to the end of time.
No wonder he blessed us when he took his leave,
for though he's far away now at the Father's side,
through his Spirit he couldn't be more near.

Quiet reflection

Prayer

Creator God,
mighty and mysterious,
awesome beyond words,
thank you for making yourself known to us in Christ –
for sharing our humanity,
walking our earth,
becoming one with us through him.
Lord Jesus Christ,
thank you for breaking down the barriers
that separate us from the Father,
for helping us not just to know but to relate to God firsthand.
Thank you that through your living, dying and rising among us
we can experience the gift of your Spirit,
your living presence deep within.
Open our eyes each day to the wonder of who you are
and of everything you have done,
and help us joyfully to worship you,
our risen, ascended Lord.
Amen.

Silent retreat

Closing comment

There's no danger, you might think, of us failing to get the bigger picture. For, unlike the apostles who had to learn as they went along, we have the benefit of hindsight: the whole story of Jesus recorded in Scripture, from his birth in Bethlehem, through to his death in Jerusalem, his resurrection from the tomb and his ascension to the Father. And alongside this we have the assistance of centuries of Christian reflection upon what that all means. Yet what picture of Jesus do we actually have? Do we see beyond the child in a manger, the teacher in Galilee, even the man on a cross? Do we see also the risen Christ, the exalted saviour, the King of kings and Lord of lords? Is our understanding of Jesus static, or one that is continually evolving, open to new horizons, fresh insights? He calls us to open our mind to the bigger picture. Don't settle for less.

Closing prayer

Lord Jesus Christ,
we praise and worship you,
for in you we see God,
his love and goodness revealed in human form;
through you his Spirit dwells within us,
daily present to lead us forward.
Thank you for all we know of your love and goodness –
for the testimony of Scripture,
witness of the Church,
and, above all, our personal experience.
Keep us eager to know more,
never assuming we have grasped the whole truth,
the complete picture.
Save us from apathy,
arrogance,
or complacency,
and teach us instead to be open to new insights,
fresh discoveries,
so that we may learn a little more about you each day.
Enlarge our vision,
broaden our horizons
and deepen our faith,
until finally we stand in your presence,
and all is revealed.
Amen.

A most amazing love

Suggested visual material

Jesus of Nazareth 2–6
The Life of Christ II and III
Oberammergau 1990
He Carries our Cross
Bread and Wine

FIRST SESSION

Introduction

What does it mean to love someone? We could spend all day discussing that question and still not exhaust it, but featuring strongly among our answers would surely be the idea of commitment, of staying true to the one we love even at cost to ourselves. When we are truly committed to someone we are ready to put *them* first and ourselves second, to risk our own well-being to safeguard theirs, to make sacrifices in order to bring them happiness. And that, according to the gospel, is the sort of love God has for us – a love that echoes our own, but that goes so very much further. Today, through readings, meditations and quiet reflection, we're going to consider four passages from the Gospels that speak of his amazing love for all.

Opening prayer

Almighty God,
speak to us of your greatness,
of your awesome creative power.
Speak of your purpose,
of your hand at work in history.
Speak of your will,
of the people you would have us be.

And speak above all of your love,
and of how it should shape every aspect of our lives.
Help us to understand not only that you *show* love,
but that you *are* love,
what it's all about,
and that, though we fail to love you,
you will go on loving us always.
Teach us more of what that means,
so that each day may be filled with grateful praise
and heartfelt joy.
Amen.

Comment

Imagine if those who love us could know our every thought, weakness and flaw. Would they love us quite so much then? Hopefully yes, but there's a real possibility such knowledge would drive a wedge between the two of us, gradually eating away at our relationship. To see the worst in someone and still to love them isn't easy, as the number of marriages that end in divorce graphically illustrates. There's a danger of subconsciously assuming the same is true with God: that he does indeed see us as we really are and is shocked as a result. So, instead of honestly opening up to him and celebrating his forgiveness, we labour under feelings of guilt, fearful of God rather than joyfully trusting him. The experience of the apostles, just one example of which is found in our next reading, shows how misplaced that is, for in Jesus they found someone who accepted them as they were, warts and all. Well aware of their faults though he was, he loved them just the same.

Music *(optional)*

O Lord, my heart is not proud (Fountain of Life) Margaret Rizza

Reading

Mark 9:30-37

Meditation of Simon the zealot

Did he need to ask what we were talking about?
Somehow I don't think so,
for he always seemed to know what we were thinking
even before we knew it ourselves.
The question was not for his benefit
but for ours –
helping us to see ourselves as we really were,
in all our weakness,
with all our faults.
He waited, mind you, till we were behind closed doors,
not wanting to embarrass us,
but we were ashamed nonetheless,
standing tongue-tied before him
like those caught hiding some guilty secret.
We were arguing, you see, over who was the greatest,
each claiming to be best,
and the higher we tried to position ourselves
the lower we stooped,
a downward spiral to the bottom.
Why do we do it?
Why do we build ourselves up by putting others down,
as if our worth must be measured at their expense?
It's the way of the world, I suppose,
but it's not *his* way,
as we were soon to learn,
for he put others first and self last,
he who was truly the greatest making himself least.
He saw the worst of us,
but also the best,
the bad,
but also the good,
sacrificing his all for people like us,
and when we think now of everything he did,
everything he gave,
we who thought ourselves so special
suddenly feel so very small.

Quiet reflection

Prayer

Gracious God,
we marvel at your love,
for we are unworthy of it –
weak,
disobedient,
foolish.
We think more highly of ourselves than we should.
We judge others,
condemning their faults
while failing to see our own.
Forgive our pride,
our arrogance,
our presumption,
and help us to recognise that we all fall short,
depending on your grace for acceptance
rather than on any merit of our own.
Teach us to put *you* first
and others before ourselves,
walking humbly in the footsteps of Christ,
who, for our sake, offered his all.
Amen.

Silence

Comment

We may be able to see people's faults yet still love them, but how about when they throw love back in our face? What then? When it is rejected, denied, betrayed, it is hard indeed to go on loving. Far easier to give way to feelings of bitterness, revenge, even hatred. Yet that's what Jesus had to endure: abandoned by so many who had followed him, including his closest disciples; denied by Peter; and, as our next reading reminds us, betrayed by Judas. Despite it all, he continued to love as much as ever, enough to continue steadfastly towards death on a cross. In him we see devotion beyond the call of duty, amazing beyond words.

Music *(optional)*

Miserere mei Allegri

Reading

John 13:21-32

Meditation of the Apostle John

We didn't have a clue,
not the first idea what was going on,
so we looked around in utter confusion.
What could he mean: one of us would betray him?
We were his friends,
devoted and loyal to a man,
or so at least we'd thought,
but it was scary how quickly that assumption changed.
Suddenly we doubted each other,
our expressions reflecting a mixture of guilt and accusation,
eyes studiously averted from too long a gaze.
I could tell some even wondered about *me*,
and why not,
for clearly our assessment of character
was not as good as we'd liked to think.
Even after Judas got up and went out,
having taken that piece of bread,
we still didn't get it,
assuming instead that he had some pressing business to attend to.
But Jesus knew what he was up to,
as he'd no doubt known all along.
What, then, of you and me?

Does he know what *we're* thinking too,
what's going on deep inside?
I rather think he may do,
and that's disconcerting, to put it mildly,
for there's so much I'd rather keep hidden,
firmly under wraps.
Would he still have time for me if he knew the worst?
Would he still welcome me as a follower if he saw who I really am?
I'd think twice in his shoes, that's for sure.
But I tell you what,
when Jesus dipped that bread into the dish and gave it to Judas,
there was no anger in his eyes,
no disgust or rejection.
Quite the opposite.
It was as though he cared for him as much as ever,
as though he valued him still as a friend.
Could that be true?
Could Jesus have died not only *because* of Judas,
but *for* him, as well?

Quiet reflection

Prayer

Almighty God,
thank you for the love you have shown in Christ –
a love that sees us as we are,
with all our weaknesses and faults,
and goes on caring;
that knows the worst about us,
coming up against rejection, denial and betrayal,
yet goes on accepting us,
faithful to the last.
Thank you that your grace is not dependent
on anything we might do,
but rests solely with you,
your nature being always to have mercy –

to forgive and restore.
With grateful hearts, we give you our praise.
Amen.

Silent retreat

SECOND SESSION

Comment

We talk of the sacrificial love of Christ, of his willingness to give everything, such was his devotion to all. But do we actually believe it? Have we grasped what it means? Have we made it our own? Our next reading reminds us of how Jesus likened himself to a shepherd, willing to lay down his life for his sheep, their welfare being his only concern. What might a shepherd listening to Jesus have made of such words?

Music *(optional)*

The love of Christ (Across the Water) Keith Duke

Reading

John 10:11-18

Meditation of a shepherd

To what lengths would I go in looking after my sheep?
That's a good question.
I'd watch over them night and day if I had to,
for it's dangerous country out there,
and there are wild animals aplenty that would make a meal of them
given half a chance.
I'd search for them too, should they be lost,
and yes, defend them if necessary, provided I was suitably armed.

But knowingly surrender my life for them?
No, I'd draw the line at that.
After all, it's sheep we're talking about, nothing more,
a way of earning a living –
keeping a roof over one's head
and money in one's pocket.
There's no room for sentimental attachment.
Would any go further?
Certainly none I know of.
A hired hand wouldn't, that's for sure;
they'd run a mile at the first whiff of danger;
and even the most dedicated among us would save their own skin first
if push came to shove.
No, I've heard of some fine shepherds in my time,
but to lay down your life for your sheep would be something else.
Could any flock be worth it?

Quiet reflection

Prayer

Lord Jesus Christ,
words cannot thank you enough for your goodness to us –
for your patience, concern and devotion.
Repeatedly we go astray,
yet you seek us out,
never resting until we are found.
We ignore your guidance,
yet you continue to call,
gently leading us back.
Though we are foolish and fickle,
naïvely following the crowd,
you stay true to us,
refusing to let us go.
For your awesome love that gave everything to bring us life,
receive our grateful praise and heartfelt worship.
Amen.

Silence

Comment

What do we need to believe about God? What are the essentials of Christian faith? The impression is sometimes given that we must assent to a long list of doctrines, and, indeed, there are many who would insist on just that. Yet is this what the gospel actually asks of us? Surely the words and actions of Jesus suggest differently, pointing to the one fundamental truth about God we must hold on to: that he is love. Such is the conclusion reached in our final reading: the celebrated words of John's Gospel 3:16. It's little wonder this verse has frequently been called the gospel in a nutshell, for indeed it is good news to live by.

Music *(optional)*

God so loved the world (The Crucifixion) Stainer

Reading

John 3:14-21

Meditation of John the Evangelist

It took me a long time to grasp it,
a lifetime of reflection on what his life, death and resurrection actually mean,
but finally the truth crystallised in a few simple words:
'God so loved the world that he gave his only Son,
so that everyone who believes in him may not perish
but will have eternal life.'
It's simple, isn't it,
yet somehow, with the best of intentions,
we make it instead so complex.
To hear some people talk,
believers included,

you'd think God feels just the opposite:
that he's concerned to judge rather than bless,
condemn rather than forgive,
punish rather than redeem.
'Believe this' they say,
'believe that',
commitment becoming a matter of jumping through the right hoops,
and woe betide us if we don't.
But that's *their* message,
not his;
a reflection of how much we struggle to accept his sheer grace,
his wholly undeserved love and pardon.
He asks merely that we *believe* in him –
no more,
no less.
Do that, and we will discover the secret of eternal life,
and, ridiculous though it may seem,
contradicting our every sense of justice and fair play,
we will receive that gift not because *we* love *God*
but because *he* loves *us*.

Quiet reflection

Prayer

Gracious God,
the words trip off the tongue easily enough –
that yours is the way of love,
that you loved the world enough to die for it,
that you are love itself –
but though we dutifully repeat such ideas
and though we accept them in theory,
in practice we struggle to accept the wonder of that message,
instead setting human limits to your grace and goodness.
Our own love is partial, flawed, conditional,
as much about ourselves as others,

and we subconsciously expect yours to be the same,
somehow dependent on us doing, saying or being the right thing.
Open our hearts to your gracious mercy that accepts us as we are –
to your love that will never let us go.
Amen.

Silent retreat

Closing comment

Love for the undeserving, the unlovely, the unlovable: that's what Jesus showed throughout his ministry, and that's what God extends to us. He's not remote or aloof from our human situation; not judgemental or vindictive, punishing us for our failure to love, or loving us only so much as we love him. There are no strings attached, no conditions: he loves us simply because it's his nature to do so. Have we grasped that truth, not just with our heads but with our hearts? Does it colour the way we live and the people we are? It should do. Amazing though such love may seem, too good to be true, it's what lies at the heart of the universe: what God is and offers to all.

Closing prayer

Lord Jesus Christ,
thank you for loving us before we first loved you,
and for continuing to love us
though we repeatedly fail to love you in return.
Though our lives deny and betray the love we profess for you,
though our response is half-hearted, inadequate and insincere,
thank you for being willing to give your all for us,
enduring suffering and death for our sake –
dying to bring us life.
Send us out in the knowledge that whoever we are,
whatever we do,
your love will never let us go.
Amen.

A most amazing man

Suggested visual material

Jesus of Nazareth 3, 4 and 6
Oberammergau 1990
He Carries our Cross

FIRST SESSION

Introduction

There have been many amazing people across the years. Names like Alexander the Great, Plato, St Augustine, Sir Isaac Newton, Isambard Kingdom Brunel, Mahatma Gandhi, Oscar Schindler, Martin Luther King and Nelson Mandela immediately spring to mind, and to those we could add innumerable others. On what grounds could we claim that Jesus is more amazing still? That's what we're going to consider today. Through a mixture of readings, meditations and quietness, we shall reflect on four people from the Gospel stories whose lives were shaped by him in different ways, each coming to recognise that he was quite unlike anyone else they'd ever known. His words and deeds, life and ministry, brought a powerful challenge that, welcome or otherwise, they couldn't evade. It's a challenge he continues to present today.

Opening prayer

Living God,
for revealing yourself in Christ, we praise you.
For coming among us through him,
walking our earth,
identifying yourself with what it means to be human,
we thank you.

For his life and ministry,
words and deeds,
death and resurrection,
and the knowledge that, through his Spirit, he is with us still,
we worship you.
Open our hearts again to his searching challenge,
healing touch
and transforming power,
and, by his grace, help us to know him better.
Amen.

Comment

Not everyone responded positively to Jesus, but such was the impact he made that none could ignore him. His radical teaching, manifest love, incredible deeds and utter integrity made waves throughout the kingdom of Judah, before long reaching the ears of King Herod himself, and troubling an already guilty conscience. He'd considered John the Baptist an astounding enough individual, yet now here was someone seemingly more astonishing still. Who was he? What did he want? And what did his coming mean? We too need to ask those questions.

Music *(optional)*

Benedictus (The New Dawn) Margaret Rizza

Reading

Mark 6:14-29

Meditation of Herod

Who is this Jesus fellow?
What sort of man is he?
Everyone's talking about him,
but none can agree who he is.

Some say he's a prophet,
others, Elijah,
but it occurred to me today that he might be something else:
my old enemy, John the baptiser.
Only he *can't* be, surely,
for I had him executed, remember –
his head brought before me on a plate –
and believe me, you don't get much more dead than that!
Could he have come back to life, though –
returned to haunt me,
get his revenge?
That's what I'm starting to wonder.
And I've a disquieting feeling I may be right,
for though I feared and resented him,
I knew also he was man of God,
speaking words of truth.
I never wanted him killed.
It was my wife who saw to that,
enticing me through that wretched daughter of hers to finish him off.
And now, it seems, I must pay for my crime . . .
Enough!
Pull yourself together man!
The dead don't come back to life,
it can't be done!
No, this Jesus is just another tub-thumper from Galilee,
a religious fanatic intent on stirring up the crowds.
Well, bring it on, that's what I say.
I'll have him despatched like John if necessary,
snuffed out once and for all –
unless, of course, this guy really can cheat the grave.
I can't see it somehow.
Can you?

Quiet reflection

Prayer

Lord Jesus Christ,
we try to evade your searching presence,
for it disturbs us,
unsettles,
asking questions we'd rather not face.
We strive to silence your voice,
to shut out unwelcome questions,
but, try though we might,
we can never succeed,
for nothing and no one can keep you down.
Teach us that though running away may seem the easy option,
in reality it is no option at all,
for we will find no peace until we face up to your challenge.
Help us, then, to be honest with ourselves
through being honest with you,
and so to find inner quietness,
the tranquillity of spirit we crave.
Amen.

Silence

Comment

If some saw in Jesus a threat to the status quo, others welcomed him with open arms, seeing in him the answer to their deepest needs, the one who could bring the hope, help and healing they craved. One such was Bartimaeus. He'd heard reports of what Jesus was doing – people made well, lives transformed – and was convinced that if he could only meet him for himself he too would find healing. His faith was to be rewarded and his life turned around.

Music *(optional)*

Open my eyes (Across the Water) Keith Duke

Reading

Mark 10:46-52

Meditation of Bartimaeus

To see again, that was wonderful enough;
to be able to look around at people and places,
gaze at the sea, the stars, the sky –
it was magical beyond words.
But Jesus did more for me than that,
opening my eyes not simply to the world about me
but also to God –
to the way, the truth and the life.
He brought healing,
in mind as well as body,
a sense of inner wholeness,
as though I was entirely made new.
For some he was just a man,
for others a teacher,
for others a threat, blasphemer,
but for me he was the Messiah,
the long-awaited Lord,
for I saw, in him, God in human form,
walking and talking among us,
his word somehow become flesh.
He'd made me well,
set me free,
and I leapt up after him,
determined to follow not just the man,
but also his way,
walking by faith as well as by sight.
I'd lived so long in darkness.
Now I'd seen his marvellous light,
and life was changed for ever.

Quiet reflection

Prayer

Loving God,
help us truly to see,
not just with our eyes but more deeply,
looking beneath the surface,
beyond appearances,
to the reality of your presence,
the wonder of who and what you are.
Help us to see Christ, through your Spirit,
in the world around us,
in one another,
in the life and witness of your Church,
in your word,
the experience of prayer
and so much more,
your light shining in the darkness,
your love illuminating our lives.
Give us insight to discern you,
wisdom to know you,
resolve to serve you
and a heart to love you,
through Jesus Christ our Lord.
Amen.

Silent retreat

SECOND SESSION

Comment

If anyone during his ministry grasped just how amazing Jesus was it was surely his disciples. They listened day after day to his teaching and witnessed firsthand his signs and wonders. Take, for example, that day when they were out on the Sea of Galilee and a storm blew up, threatening to drown them all. It was astonishing enough that Jesus could lie back in the boat, apparently totally relaxed; more astounding still that he could calm the wind and waves. Yet even that was to pale into insignificance compared to the transformation he would bring to their lives, and that of so many others.

Music *(optional)*

Tide change (Across the Water) Keith Duke

Reading

Mark 4:35-41

Meditation of the Apostle John

We were petrified,
quite simply, scared out of our wits,
for the wind and waves grew fiercer by the minute,
tossing our boat about like so much driftwood.
Could we have ridden it out?
I don't think so,
for we were taking in water by the bucket-load,
and, frantically though we tried to bale it out,
it was only a matter of time before we capsized.
What was Jesus doing, you ask?
Well, believe it or not, he was sleeping!
I *know*, it sounds crazy doesn't it,
and if *you're* surprised, how do you think *we* felt?
We were used to the sea, remember,
experienced fishermen,
but this storm was something else,
as savage as any we'd encountered.
Yet while we lurched around in panic,
Jesus bedded down there in the stern of the boat
as though we were taking a gentle cruise,
his face as peaceful as the proverbial baby.
Even when we woke him there was no sign of fear –
just that serene, almost surreal, air of calm,

and the next moment the storm was stilled,
as if it had never been.
A relief, you'd think,
and so it was, eventually,
but I tell you what:
for a time afterwards we were more scared than we'd been before,
not of the water but of *him*,
for who or what gave him such power and authority?
We'd seen him forgive sins,
heal the sick,
restore the broken,
but now here he was changing not just people
but the world itself,
even the wind and waves obeying him.
He was an amazing character, we knew that already,
but we were beginning to realise he was much more,
for, dare I say it,
no ordinary man could do such things –
only God!

Quiet reflection

Prayer

Lord Jesus Christ,
still the storms in our lives –
of fear and anxiety,
of sudden crises,
of tragedy, trauma and trouble.
Still the storms in our world –
of injustice and intolerance,
of manmade and natural disaster,
of hatred, bloodshed and war.
Through your divine power, reach out wherever life brings turmoil
and calm the waves,
bringing true and lasting peace,
rest for our souls.
Amen.

Silence

Comment

What sort of person would you get up and follow without a moment's hesitation? Who, if anyone, would you abandon a settled way of life for and step out into the unknown? It would take someone pretty amazing to inspire that, someone with qualities that clearly set them apart from others. And if allegiance to that person led you to face hostility, persecution, even eventually to lose your life for their cause, you might be forgiven for thinking you made the wrong choice. Yet although Judas came to just such a conclusion, the remaining apostles reckoned otherwise. Demanding, difficult, dangerous though discipleship may have been, they considered it also special beyond words. In Jesus they had found someone who was not only different but also unique: the fulfilment of their hopes and prayers, someone able to quench their spiritual thirst, a man who somehow revealed to them the very face of God. What else could they do but follow, wherever it might lead?

Music *(optional)*

I am a pilgrim (Heavenly Light) Geoffrey Nobes

Reading

Mark 8:27-38

Meditation of Simon Peter

I thought he was just curious, at the start,
interested to hear what the crowds were saying about him –
after all, wouldn't you have wanted to know in his shoes?
So we told him what rumours were circulating:
'Some say John the Baptist,
others Elijah,
others Jeremiah, or one of the prophets.'

He smiled at that,
clearly unsurprised,
but then he turned the question on us.
'What about you?' he said.
'Who do *you* say I am?'
It was a challenge that changed our mood completely,
for suddenly he was asking not simply about *others*
but about *us* –
where *we* stood,
what *we* thought!
We'd been content until then to stay in the wings,
observing rather than observed,
watching safely from the sidelines,
but the time had come to decide.
No longer could we simply dip our feet in,
testing the waters;
we had to take the plunge,
sink or swim –
and, put like that, I for one had no hesitation.
We knew already he was special –
that had been clear to us from the beginning –
for he had an air about him,
almost an aura, you might say,
that set him apart,
speaking of authority,
wisdom,
love;
in short, of God.
That's why I'd followed in the first place,
attracted and intrigued,
and though my understanding was far from complete,
I'd glimpsed enough to grasp
that he offered what no one else could begin to –
a hope, love and life unlike anything I'd known before –
so I opened my heart,
and offered my commitment.
It's not all been plain sailing,
don't think that.

On the contrary, it's been hard sometimes,
testing me to the limit.
But it's been wonderful, too,
the best decision I've ever made,
for not only have I followed *him* on *his* journey,
he's also become part of *mine*!

Quiet reflection

Prayer

Lord Jesus Christ,
keep our faith real,
fresh,
vibrant,
alive.
May it be about *us* and *you* –
about a personal relationship,
a living, daily experience of your love.
Save us from second-hand discipleship –
from commitment based on what we've been told to believe,
on past confessions of faith,
or on what we've gathered about you from others.
Meet with us each day, through your Spirit.
Speak your word,
issue your call,
and help us to respond.
Amen.

Silent retreat

Closing comment

There have indeed been many amazing people throughout the course of history, people whom we rightly remember and salute. But have any made quite the impact of Jesus? Have any changed the lives of so many people over so many centuries? Have any taught with such simplicity yet such searching authority? Have any brought such joy and hope? Have any hung on a cross and been sealed in a tomb, only to appear again, risen and victorious? Have any brought the promise of light in darkness, joy out of sorrow, life beyond death? How is it that someone executed as a common criminal in a far-flung outpost of the Roman empire has had such a profound influence on countless lives across the world from that day to this? For anyone to do that, they must be amazing indeed.

Closing prayer

Lord Jesus Christ,
go with us in the daily round of life.
Continue to speak to us,
teaching us more of your way.
Continue to bless us,
bringing joy out of sorrow,
hope out of despair.
Continue to nurture, guide, comfort and support,
offering a light to our path in our journey through life.
Lord Jesus Christ,
continue to amaze us through who and what you are.
Amen.

Appendix

Visual resources

As indicated in the Foreword, few visual resources that I'm aware of are currently in print, but you should be able to order at least some of those listed below through your local library or Diocesan Resource Centre. As well as the collections mentioned, I have occasionally used slides of the Holy Land, particularly, for example, scenes of the wilderness to accompany meditations on Jesus' temptation or John the Baptist preaching in the desert. It's worth also looking online for other images, such as Davis Art Images (see http://www.davis-art.com/Portal/DAI/SlideSets_Default.aspx?curPage=ProductDetails&ModelNumber=LI FA1; Davis Publications, Inc., 50 Portland Street, Worcester, MA 01608), for portrayals of Jesus in art. For me, still one of the most powerful visual depictions of Jesus is that in the six-set pack of 144 slides based on the television series *Jesus of Nazareth* directed by Franco Zeffirelli, produced by the Bible Society.

(Note: An asterisk indicates that the resource is no longer commercially available. Those not marked are still in print, as far I know.)

*Jesus of Nazareth 1: Jesus – Birth & Childhood**
*Jesus of Nazareth 2: Jesus – Begins his Ministry**
*Jesus of Nazareth 3: Jesus – Heals**
*Jesus of Nazareth 4: Jesus – Cares**
*Jesus of Nazareth 5: Jesus – In the Last Week**
*Jesus of Nazareth 6: Jesus – Trial to Resurrection**
Colour transparencies from the TV series directed by Franco Zeffirelli. Produced by the Bible Society.

The Life of Christ I (Annunciation, nativity, and childhood)
The Life of Christ II (Christ's public ministry)
The Life of Christ III (The crucifixion)
The Life of Christ IV (The resurrection)
Slides focusing on the life of Jesus, as 'seen through the eyes of the artist', produced by Visual Publications, The Green, Northleach, Cheltenham, Gloucestershire GL54 3EX.

*Jesus, the Child**
A cartoon slide-set produced in conjunction with a Ladybird Bible Book primarily aimed at children. Was produced by the Scripture Union.

*Come let us adore**
A series of 27 slides on the nativity. Was produced by Audio Visual Productions UK.

*The Parables of Jesus**
A slide-set primarily aimed at children. Was produced by the National Christian Education Council.

Oberammergau 1990
A sequence of 36 slides from the Oberammergau Passion Plays, produced by Huber, Drosselstrasse 7, D-8100 Garmisch-Partenkirchen, Germany.

Man of the Cross
A slide-sound presentation (code 70P326), also available as a set of 15 posters (code 73P262), using a variety of artistic media, including photography, vividly portraying the Way of the Cross. Produced by St Paul Multimedia Productions, 199 Kensington High Street, London W8 6BA.

*He Carries our Cross**
An audio-visual programme for liturgy, prayer and reflection, including slides of line-sketches, focusing on the events of the Passion under two subsections: (a) Journey to Jerusalem, and (b) Journey to the Cross. Was produced by St Paul Audio Visual Productions.

*Bread and Wine**
Pictures of the elements of the Eucharist, particularly suitable for meditations on the Last Supper. Was produced for the Church Pastoral Aid Society by Falcon Audio Visual Aids.

*St Paul**
A radiovision slide set consisting of 45 picture slides. Was produced by the BBC.

Other Nick Fawcett books you'll love

Daily Prayer
1500601

Daily Reflections
1501284

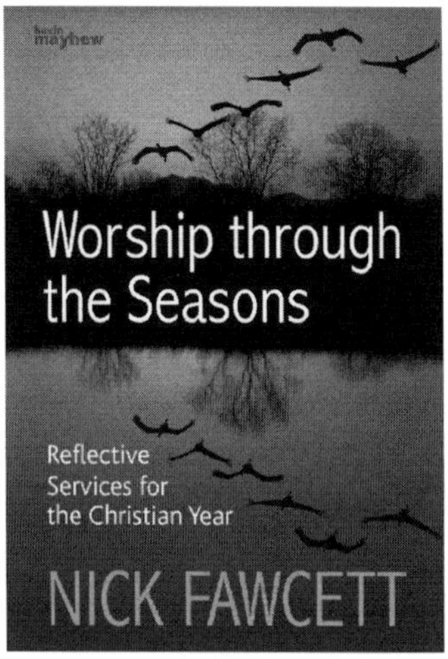

Worship through the
Seasons - Paperback
1501283

Reflective Services for
Advent and Christmas
1500454